PARTY PIECES

PARTY PIECES

50 food ideas for successful parties

Elizabeth Wolf-Cohen

Photographs by
Amanda Heywood

WHITECAP
BOOKS

This edition first published in 1997 by Whitecap Books

Whitecap Books
351 Lynn Avenue
North Vancouver
British Columbia
Canada V7J 2C4

© Anness Publishing Limited 1997

Produced by Anness Publishing Inc.
27 West 20th Street
New York, NY 10011

ISBN 1 55110 666 3

Publisher: Joanna Lorenz
Project Editor: Joanne Rippin
Designer: Alan Marshall
Photographer: Amanda Heywood

Typeset by MC Typeset Ltd, Rochester, Kent
Printed and bound in Hong Kong

1 3 5 7 9 10 8 6 4 2

CONTENTS

Introduction   **6**

NUTS & NIBBLES   **20**

QUICK & EASY   **30**

SUBSTANTIAL SNACKS   **50**

RICH & LAVISH   **68**

EAST MEETS WEST   **82**

Index   **96**

INTRODUCTION

A party is the perfect way to show off some of the prettiest and tastiest foods. And, because most of the preparation work can be done in advance, this kind of entertaining is generally much less demanding than formal dinner parties.

Planning the menu is the most enjoyable part of the preparations—informal or formal, large or small, close friends or business associates, the occasion will help you decide the right scale and approach. Time of day and the length of your guests' stay will also influence your arrangements—a few drinks with friends before going to a movie will require only one or two nibbles, whereas a three-hour party will obviously need something more substantial.

Small pieces of food that can be eaten with one hand make the best party foods (remember each guest will be holding a glass in one hand). Plan to have something to serve the moment people arrive, maybe a tray of crudités with a dip, as this gives guests something to focus on and helps them to relax. Move on to something hot when most people have arrived, then alternate between hot and cold, finishing with something warm or sweet. Serving sweet food is an ideal, subtle way of suggesting that the party is drawing to a close.

In this book, you will find easy recipes for simple roasted nuts and herbed olives, as well as more elaborate concoctions, such as wild rice pancakes with smoked salmon nests. But remember, with a little imagination almost any food can be adapted to party-sized pieces.

Condiments

Many different condiments can be used to put together a quick dip or snack at a moment's notice. Tomato ketchup and horseradish sauce can be stirred together with mayonnaise and a squeeze of lemon, to use as a dip for shrimp or hard-boiled eggs. Or, add chopped green onion to soy sauce and mango chutney and spoon onto Asian shrimp crackers for another instant snack. The variations are endless—just use your imagination.

Barbecue sauce
Bottled barbecue sauces are ideal for adding an outdoor flavor to broiled foods. They can be spread on pieces of meat or vegetables, which are then broiled and skewered onto toothpicks.

Capers
The little buds of the Mediterranean caper bush, preserved in vinegar, these add an extra piquancy to sauces and salads. They are especially good on pizzas and salads.

Chili sauce
This bottled sauce is widely available in supermarkets and Chinese grocers. It gives a warm sweet-spicy taste to most foods and sauces. Use in dips and marinades.

Corn relish
This sweet-and-tangy relish for hamburgers can also be used to top slices of cold chicken, beef, or ham, or hard-boiled eggs.

Dijon mustard
Indispensable for salad dressings, sauces, and dips, as well as to spread on meats and cheeses. It is sometimes flavored with green peppercorns or other aromatics.

English mustard
Sold already made up or as powder to be mixed to a paste. This is a traditional relish for accompanying beef, ham, and cheese.

Grainy mustard
The best known grainy mustard is from the region near Meaux, France, although other traditional whole-grain mustards are also available. It is delicious with ham and pâtés.

Horseradish sauce
This hot, spicy sauce can be bought as a relish, or "creamed" which makes it slightly milder. Often served with roast beef, it is also perfect with smoked and oily fish, chicken, and other seafood.

Mango chutney
Traditionally served with spicy food, this chutney is also delicious with cheese, ham, chicken mayonnaise, or egg salad.

Mayonnaise
A good-quality mayonnaise is indispensable. Use it as a dip or a spread, or to bind chopped hard-boiled eggs or chicken into toppings for toasts to serve as a quick canapé. Making your own is worth the effort.

Plum sauce
Made from plums, apricots, garlic, chilies, sugar, vinegar, and flavorings, this thick, sweet Cantonese condiment makes an ideal dip for Chinese-style snacks, or base for a barbecue sauce.

Soy sauce
This sauce is the basis of many Chinese-style dips and sauces. (Light soy sauce is more common than dark, but it is saltier, dilute it with a little water.) Add chopped green onions and cilantro for an easy dipping sauce.

Tartar sauce
This is the standard sauce for fried fish and shellfish. It is delicious with fish cakes. A mixture of mayonnaise, sweet gherkins, green onions, capers, and vinegar; try making your own.

Tomato chutney
Chutneys of all kinds make a tasty accompaniment to cold meats, savory pastries and salamis, as well as cheeses and cold broiled or grilled vegetables.

Tomato ketchup
This universal condiment can be used in barbecue sauces and marinades or spread on toast and topped with cheese or sliced meats for a quick canapé.

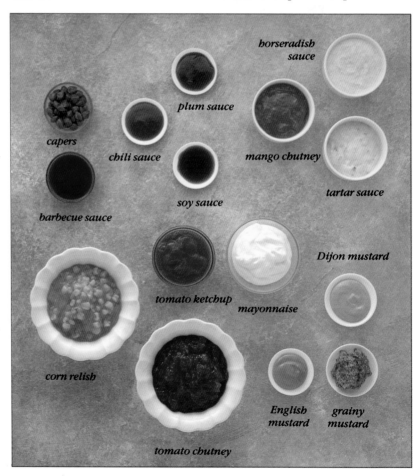

capers

chili sauce

barbecue sauce

corn relish

plum sauce

soy sauce

tomato ketchup

tomato chutney

horseradish sauce

mango chutney

tartar sauce

Dijon mustard

mayonnaise

English mustard

grainy mustard

Herbs

Fresh herbs can be used generously in party foods, as they provide fresh flavor and interest to many different dishes. They also make a simple but elegant garnish. Use the same herb that you use in a recipe to garnish the serving plate—this provides a hint of what's in the food.

If you are lucky enough to have a garden, or even a window box, grow your own herbs so you will always have some to hand. If you can't grow your own, choose from the extensive range of fresh herbs available from supermarkets.

flat-leaf parsley

mint

watercress

lemongrass

bay

thyme

chives

dill

cilantro

oregano

basil

Basil
The warm, spicy scent of basil epitomizes the flavors of the Mediterranean. Use it with tomatoes, summer salads, vegetable dishes, and, of course, in pesto with pine nuts and Parmesan cheese.

Bay
This leaf of the laurel family gives a delicate flavor to soups, casseroles, and pâtés. Bay leaves make a pretty garnish which will stay fresh for hours.

Chives
A member of the onion family, the mild flavor is wonderful with almost anything, but especially in herb butters, cheeses, cream sauces, egg dishes, and, of course, with sour cream on baked potatoes.

Cilantro
This wonderfully aromatic herb is used in Mexican, Chinese, Indian, Greek, Turkish, and North African cooking, to add subtle spiciness to dishes such as stir-fries, curries, and hummus.

Dill
Most often used in fish dishes, such as the Scandinavian *gravlax*, the slightly aniseed flavor of dill is also delicious with eggs, potatoes, chicken, and cucumber, and in soft cheese recipes. Its soft, fernlike leaves make a lovely garnish.

Flat-leaf parsley
Sometimes called Italian parsley, this variety has a slightly stronger flavor than curly parsley. It adds interest and color to almost any savory dish, especially vegetables and fish, and makes a beautiful garnish.

Lemongrass
The stem of this lemon-scented broad-leaved grass is used in Southeast Asian dishes, especially those from Thailand. If you cannot find it, substitute a little freshly grated lemon peel.

Mint
This herb, with its many varieties, gives a fresh tingle to fish, goat cheeses, and salads, and is wonderful in dips. It is used extensively in Middle Eastern cooking.

Oregano
Sometimes called wild majoram, this has a powerful flavor used in tomato sauces and with vegetable dishes of the southern Mediterranean and Greece.

Thyme
This intensely aromatic herb is used in lamb or chicken dishes. It is also good in tomato sauces and vegetable dishes, and is an integral part of a bouquet garni.

Watercress
Technically, this is a vegetable and a member of the mustard family. Its peppery flavor is particularly good in sandwiches or with egg and fish, and it can be used as an attractive garnish.

Spices

Spices are an important part of all kinds of cooking, but are especially useful in party food to provide extra flavor and stimulate appetites. Store all spices, ground or whole, in airtight jars, away from heat or light, to prevent loss of color and flavor. If possible, grind your own freshly each time you use some, especially pepper and nutmeg.

Aniseed
This Mediterranean seed is used in breads and pastries, as well as in fish dishes and marinades.

Cardamom pods
Used in Indian, Arab, and North African stews and other dishes, the sweetish fragrant flavor is also popular in German and Scandinavian baking. Crush the pods with a rolling pin to release the flavor. Cardamom is also available ground, but in this form, loses its flavor quickly.

Cayenne pepper
This is the ground red powder of a very pungent dried red chili. It can be used sparingly in a variety of dishes and sauces to add piquancy and warmth. It has the advantage of being virtually invisible.

Chili flakes
These flakes are crushed hot, red chilies and include pieces of the chilies as well as the seeds. These are very strong, but, used sparingly, make an ideal addition to soups, stews, marinades, and sauces.

Cinnamon
Available in sticks or ground, its warm flavor is well known in baking. The sticks can also be used in spicy meat or vegetable stews and in poaching syrups for fruits and in custards.

Coriander seeds
The small, round seeds of the coriander plant have a warm, mildly spicy flavor when roasted. They are used in Indian, Moroccan, and Southeast Asian cooking, as well as in pickling and marinades.

Cumin
This mildly piquant seed has a sweetish flavor and intense aroma. Used in many North African dishes, it can be bought as seeds or ground.

Dried mustard powder
This is the traditional English mustard, based on ground brown and white mustard seeds. Mixed to a paste with cold water, vinegar or milk, it is a traditional accompaniment for beef, ham, and cheeses. The strong, but smooth pungent flavor is ideal for fish, egg, and vegetable dishes, as well as many sauces.

Dried gingerroot
This can be grated into many dishes to give a hot and spicy, yet refreshing, flavor. Fresh gingerroot can replace dried if peeled and then chopped or grated finely. Delicious in many Chinese, Indian, and Middle Eastern dishes.

Fennel seeds
The seeds of the fennel bulb have a sweet, aniseed flavor. They can be used in baking and to flavor soups and stews. They can also be used instead of aniseed.

Fresh chilies
Technically, chilies are a vegetable from the capsicum family. Used sparingly they add a lively heat to all kinds of dishes, especially curries and salsas.

Garlic
Actually a member of the onion family, garlic is most often used as a flavoring, although fresh sweet garlic can also be cooked as a vegetable. In small quantities, its sweet, pungent flavor enhances almost any savoury dish.

Hot red chilies
These small, intensely hot chilies are frequently used in many Thai and other southeast Asian dishes. Use sparingly.

Mustard seeds
The seeds of the mustard plant impart a hot, pungent taste and aroma to any marinade or pickled dish. Crush lightly to release the flavor.

Nutmeg
Besides being a baking essential, a little freshly grated nutmeg adds a warm, sweet, nutty flavor to pastas, white sauces, and cheese dishes.

Paprika
This red powder, ground from dried ripe capsicums, can be mild or hot. It is used in Austrian and Hungarian cooking, as well as in many Spanish dishes. It can be used as a pretty garnish on egg dishes or creamy sauces.

Peppercorns
Green peppercorns are the unripe fruit of the *Piper nigrum* vine. They have a milder flavor than the black peppercorns, which are small pickled green peppercorns, that have been dried whole. One of the most important spices, freshly ground black pepper is intensely aromatic and mildly spicy.

Poppy seeds
The tiny, hard slate-blue seeds of the opium poppy are used mostly in baking. Try them in salad dressings and noodle dishes for a slightly sweet, nutty flavor.

Sea salt
The large white crystals of dried sea salt have a pure salty flavor and can be used in cooking or on the table. Use sea salt as a dry dip for quail eggs or sprinkle it over salad greens.

Sesame seeds
These tiny white seeds are used in oriental cooking and lend a subtle, savory flavor and crunch to fried foods. They also provide an attractive nutty finish to breads and pastries.

Star anise
This pretty star-shaped spice is the fruit and seed pod of an evergreen tree. It is an important part of Chinese cooking, imparting a deep aniseed or licorice flavor. Use in marinades and in duck and pork dishes.

fresh chilies

sesame seeds

dried gingerroot

star anise

nutmeg

cinnamon

cayenne pepper

poppy seeds

cardamom pods

dried mustard powder

coriander seeds

chili flakes

min

fennel seeds

hot red chilies

aniseed

peppercorns

sea salt

garlic

mustard seeds

paprika

Kitchen Cupboard Nibbles

It is always a good idea to keep a variety of nuts and other nibbles in the cupboard. Often a few potato chips, peanuts, or olives are all you need to offer with drinks before going out or before a meal. Look in specialty gourmet stores and ethnic markets for unusual nibbles.

Bread sticks (grissini)
Stand these in a pitcher for an easy snack on their own or with something to dip into, or spread each with a little herb butter.

Bombay mix
Commercially prepared versions of this Indian snack are sold in Asian grocery stores. It is a mixture of fried nuts, legumes, and other nibbles flavored with curry spices—perfect before an Indian meal.

Cheese straws
These cheese-flavored twists of flaky pastry look pretty and make a tasty snack.

Dried apricots
Dried fruit makes an interesting alternative to salty, savory nibbles. Also, try dried peaches, dates, prunes, figs, and banana chips for healthy snacks.

Dried cranberries
Popular as a baking ingredient, these are also good on their own or mixed with dried cherries.

Gherkins
Little sweet pickled gherkins are delicious as an appetizer, as well as being low in calories.

Green olives
A wide variety of olives is available in supermarkets. For a party snack, the pitted variety are the most convenient. Spanish olives are often stuffed with tiny pieces of red pimiento, almonds, or anchovies.

Honey roast cashews
These biscuit-flavored nuts have a slightly sweet, honey coating.

Japanese rice crackers
These puffs of rice with peanuts inside or wrapped with dried seaweed, these make a sophisticated nibble and look very attractive.

Macadamia nuts
These nuts come from Hawaii and Australia and have a delicate, slightly sweet flavor. They are expensive but delicious.

Pistachio nuts
Always popular these pretty green nuts are sold still in their shells. Don't forget to provide little dishes for the empty shells.

Pita chips
These tiangles of pita bread brushed with oil and sprinkled with herbs, and baked until crisp and golden, provide a crunchy snack.

Popcorn
Plain popcorn makes a healthy, low-calorie snack. Tossed with butter or oil and salt, it is even more delicious, but more calorific. Various flavors of popped corn can be found in most supermarkets.

Potato chips
Universally popular, chips come in a bewildering variety of flavors.

Pretzel sticks
A delicious crunchy snack, these salty sticks are handy to keep as a standby, and easy to serve.

Shrimp crackers
These commercially-made pale puffs are crunchy and scented with a shrimp flavor. They are often served in Chinese or Thai restaurants.

Tortilla chips
Triangles of fried corn, these little tortillas are ideal with a drink or cocktail such as a margarita. They are also sold with chili flavoring.

shrimp crackers

Japanese rice crackers

popcorn

macadamia nuts

cheese straws

pita crisps

tortilla chips

dried apricots

Bombay-mix

gherkins

green olives

pistachio nuts

potato chips

dried cranberries

bread sticks (grissini)

pretzel sticks

honey roast cashews

Drinks

Without drinks there is no party, so you need to offer something—even if it is only lemonade! No one expects your house to be a bar or cocktail lounge, and a small party can probably be managed with a bottle or two of white wine in the refrigerator, maybe a bottle of red, and some soft drinks and bottled water.

Deciding what to serve and quantities can be tricky. Remember that spirits, or hard drinks, don't go off, so it is better to overestimate than to run out. You might choose to offer only wine or Champagne before a small dinner party; or you could set up a small bar, with one or two spirits, such as gin or vodka and a sherry, as well as wine. For a bigger party, a bar with mixers for two or three cocktails could help set a theme. Your budget will probably be the deciding factor but, whatever you offer, always have lots of water, soft drinks, and fruit juice for non-drinkers and children.

One bottle of wine will fill six average glasses, but if you are only serving wine or Champagne, allow half a bottle per person. Most people drink white wine at a cocktail party, but plan on one-third drinking red. By far the easiest plan is to decide what you want to serve and offer a filled glass to your guests as they enter. Champagne is very festive and creates an instant party atmosphere. Almost nobody refuses it, and there are lots of other good bubbly substitutes

available, such as Italian proseccos, Spanish cavas, and New World sparkling Chardonnays. Serve on its own or mixed with a little raspberry or black-currant liqueur (a *kir*), orange juice (mimosa), or peach juice (a Bellini); this will also provide more drinks per bottle.

If refrigerator space is at a premium, fill a bathtub, sink, large cooler, or even a clean garbage can with lots of ice to cool the wine, water, and soft drinks. Allow two glasses per person, as people tend to abandon their glasses as they move around. Wine stores often lend glasses if you buy a case of wine, or buy extra glasses to keep on hand specifically for parties. A standard white-wine, or tulip, glass can be used for just about anything. If it is a large party, set up an extra wine station in another part of the room, with a few bottles on ice and some extra glasses; this helps prevent a bottle-neck at your primary bar or in the kitchen.

Remember, the most important thing is for you and your guests to relax and enjoy yourselves, so keep everything simple.

Garnishes

Garnishes on party food need to last longer than those on a dinner plate, which are eaten immediately—so keep them simple. Green, yellow, and red tend to bring out the color in foods, so stick to what looks best.

LEMON/CUCUMBER TWISTS

1 With a canelle knife, remove strips of peel down the length of the lemon or cucumber. Slice thinly, then make a slit from one edge to the center of each slice.

2 Twist the sides in opposite directions to form a twist.

RADISH FANS

1 Using a sharp knife, cut lengthwise slits, leaving the stem end intact.

2 Gently push the radish to one side, causing the slices to fan out.

CHILI FLOWERS

1 Slit the chilies lengthwise and gently scrape out any seeds. Cut lengthwise into as many strips as possible, leaving the stem ends intact.

2 Drop the chilies into a bowl of iced water and refrigerate several hours until curled. (The iced water causes the strips to curl back.)

GREEN ONION POMPOMS

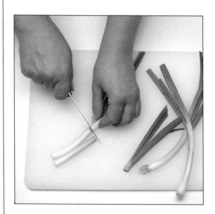

1 Trim the green onions and cut each into pieces about 3 inches long.

2 Using a small knife, cut as many slits lengthwise as possible, leaving the root end intact. Drop into a bowl of iced water and refrigerate for several hours or overnight until curled. (The iced water causes the strips to curl back.)

Roasting Sweet Peppers

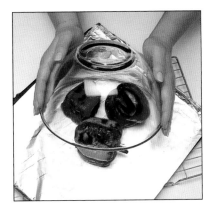 

1 Place the peppers on a foil-lined cookie sheet and broil until blackened and blistered on all sides, turning occasionally. Cover the peppers with a large bowl or place in a plastic bag and seal, until cool.

2 Using a sharp knife, peel off the charred skins. Cut the peppers into strips, removing the core and seeds but reserving any juices.

Lining Small Tartlet Pans

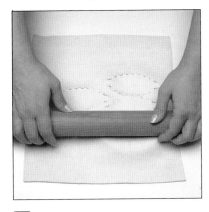 

1 Roll out the dough as the recipe directs. Arrange the tartlet pans close to each other on the counter. Roll the dough loosely back onto the rolling pin, then roll out over the pans. Roll the rolling pin firmly over the dough to cut the edges.

2 Using both thumbs, carefully press the dough into the bottom and up the sides of each pan.

Using a Canelle Knife

1 Holding the fruit or vegetable in one hand, pull the canelle knife along the surface at regular intervals to create grooves in the surface.

2 Cut the fruit or vegetable horizontally to make pretty, ridged slices.

Easy Sauces and Spreads

MAYONNAISE

Homemade mayonnaise is well worth making to use as a spread or dip. If you like, add some herbs along with the egg yolks. Remember mayonnaise is made with raw egg yolks, so use fresh eggs from a good supplier. Raw eggs are not suitable for young children, the elderly, or pregnant women.

Makes about 1¹/₂ cups

INGREDIENTS
2 egg yolks
1 tablespoon Dijon mustard
1 tablespoon white wine vinegar
1¼ cups olive oil or half olive oil and
    half sunflower oil

I Put the egg yolks in the bowl of a food processor. Add the mustard and vinegar and process for 10 seconds to blend.

2 With the machine running, gradually pour the oil through the feed tube until a smooth paste forms. Pour into a jar and spoon a little more oil over to seal the surface. Cover tightly and refrigerate, where it will keep for up to one week, or freeze in smaller quantities.

EASY PESTO SAUCE

Pesto is a delicious sauce which can be used on its own or stirred into sour cream or mayonnaise to make a quick dip. Use a good-quality olive oil.

Makes about 1¹/₄ cups

INGREDIENTS
about 2 cups fresh basil leaves
1 to 2 garlic cloves
3 tablespoons freshly grated Parmesan
    cheese
3 tablespoons pine nuts, lightly
    toasted
salt
freshly ground black pepper
4 to 6 tablespoons virgin olive oil,
    plus extra for sealing

I Put the basil leaves, garlic, Parmesan cheese, and pine nuts in the bowl of a food processor. Season with salt and pepper and process until well blended, scraping down the side of the bowl once or twice.

2 With the machine running, gradually pour the oil through the feed tube in a steady stream until all the oil is incorporated and the sauce is thickened. Add 1 to 2 tablespoons boiling water and process briefly to blend. Will keep in the refrigerator for up to 3 days.

QUICK TAPENADE

Tapenade is an olive spread served in the Mediterranean as a tasty snack spread on toasts, or stirred into soups and stews. Keep it on hand for quick *crostini* or stir into soft cheese for an easy spread or dip.

Makes about 1 cup

INGREDIENTS
⅔ cup kalamata, or other oil-cured ripe olives, pitted
1 to 2 garlic cloves
1 tablespoon capers, rinsed and drained
3 tablespoons virgin olive oil, plus extra for sealing
2 to 4 anchovy fillets, drained
juice of ½ lemon
chopped fresh cilantro

1 Put all the ingredients, except the cilantro into the bowl of a food processor and process until finely chopped, scraping down the side of the bowl once or twice.

2 Spoon into a small bowl and stir in the chopped cilantro. Spoon a little extra olive oil over to seal. Cover and refrigerate up to 2 weeks.

BASIC TOMATO SAUCE

This sauce can be used as the base for pasta or vegetable sauces, as a pizza base, or a seasoned dip. Use ripe tomatoes with lots of flavor and your favorite herbs.

Makes about 1⅓ cups

INGREDIENTS
2 tablespoons olive oil
1 large onion, chopped
1 to 2 garlic cloves, chopped
½ teaspoon chopped fresh thyme leaves or ¼ teaspoon dried thyme
1 to 2 bay leaves
6 to 8 ripe plum tomatoes
¼ cup water or stock
1 to 2 teaspoons chopped fresh herbs

1 In a large skillet or saucepan, heat the olive oil over medium heat. Add the onions and cook for 5 to 7 minutes, stirring frequently, until softened. Add the garlic, thyme, and bay leaves and cook for 1 minute longer. Stir in the tomatoes and water or stock. Bring to a boil and cook, uncovered, for 15 to 20 minutes over medium heat until most of the liquid has evaporated and the sauce has thickened.

2 Pour into the bowl of a food processor and process until smooth. Press through a strainer to remove any skin and seeds, then stir in the herbs. Cool and refrigerate for up to 4 days.

Hot Pepper Pecans

These nuts are easy to make and can be prepared up to a week ahead, then stored in an airtight container.

Makes about 3 cups

INGREDIENTS
1 tablespoon butter
1 tablespoon sesame oil
3 cups pecan halves
1 to 2 tablespoons soy sauce
2 to 3 dashes hot-pepper sauce, or
    to taste
1 tablespoon clear honey (optional)

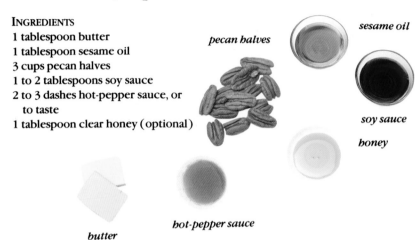

pecan halves

sesame oil

soy sauce

honey

hot-pepper sauce

butter

1 Preheat the oven to 300°F. Put the butter and oil on a medium-size baking tray and heat in the oven until the butter melts. Remove and swirl to blend. Stir in the pecans until well coated, then toast them in the oven for 30 minutes, stirring once or twice.

2 Sprinkle the soy sauce over the nuts, then add a few dashes of hot-pepper sauce and the honey, if using. Toss the nuts until well coated, then allow to cool. Store in an airtight container.

Easy Nachos

This Tex-Mex specialty, a spicy cheese snack that can be made in minutes, is always popular.

Makes 24

INGREDIENTS
2 or 3 fresh or pickled jalapeño or
    other medium-hot chili peppers
24 large tortilla chips
scant 2 cups grated Cheddar cheese
2 green onions, finely chopped
sour cream, to serve (optional)

chili peppers

tortilla chips

sour cream

grated Cheddar cheese

green onions

COOK'S TIP

When handling chilies, wear rubber gloves and be sure to wash your knife and cutting board well, as the chili oils can irritate skin and eyes.

1 With a small sharp knife, split the chili peppers and remove the seeds (the hottest part). Slice thinly.

2 Preheat the oven to 425°F. Arrange the tortilla chips in a single layer on a large baking tray lined with foil. Sprinkle a little grated cheese onto each tortilla chip and top with a slice of chili and a few green onions. Bake for about 5 minutes until golden and bubbling. Serve hot with sour cream, if you like.

Spicy Microwave Poppadums

This is a wonderfully easy way to prepare a spicy snack. Poppadums are Indian and traditionally fried, but this method is much lighter.

Makes 6 or 12

INGREDIENTS
6 poppadums, broken in half if you
   wish
vegetable oil for brushing
cayenne pepper or chili powder

poppadums

vegetable oil

chili powder

1 Lay the poppadums on a counter and brush each one lightly with a little vegetable oil. Sprinkle with a pinch of cayenne pepper or chili powder.

2 Arrange 2 to 4 poppadums (depending on the size of your microwave) on paper towels and microwave on High (100%) for 40 to 60 seconds. Serve immediately.

VARIATION

If you don't have a microwave, you can make the same snack by using poppadums which can be broiled, and following the directions on the package after step one. Look for boxes of flat poppadums in Asian grocery stores.

Hot-and-Spicy Popcorn

This is an ideal nibble for a crowd. Making your own popcorn is easy, but you can use the popped, store-bought variety if you like. Adjust the chili powder to suit your taste.

Makes about 12 cups

INGREDIENTS
½ cup vegetable oil, plus extra for
   popping
1 cup unpopped popcorn
2 to 3 garlic cloves, crushed
1 to 2 teaspoons chili powder
   (according to taste)
pinch cayenne pepper
salt

vegetable oil

popcorn

garlic cloves

chili powder

cayenne pepper

1 In a large heavy saucepan, heat the extra oil, then pop the corn according to the manufacturer's directions.

2 In a small saucepan, combine the oil, the garlic cloves, chili powder, and cayenne pepper. Cook over low heat for about 5 minutes, stirring occasionally. Remove the garlic cloves with a slotted spoon, then pour the flavored oil over the popped popcorn. Toss well to combine and season with salt to taste. Serve warm or at room temperature.

VARIATION

For Parmesan Popcorn, omit the chili powder and salt and proceed as above. After pouring over the seasoned oil, add 4 to 6 tablespoons freshly grated Parmesan cheese, and toss well.

Celery Sticks with Roquefort

This delicious filling can also be made with English Stilton or any other blue cheese. Diluted with a little milk or cream, it also makes a delicious dip.

Makes about 45

INGREDIENTS
7 ounces Roquefort or other blue
    cheese, softened
1¼ cups lowfat cream cheese
2 green onions, finely chopped
black pepper
1 to 2 tablespoons milk
1 celery head
chopped walnuts or hazelnuts, to
    garnish

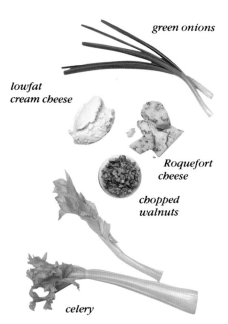

green onions

*lowfat
cream cheese*

*Roquefort
cheese*

*chopped
walnuts*

celery

I With a fork, crumble the Roquefort in a bowl. Put in a food processor with the cream cheese, green onions, and black pepper. Process until smooth, scraping down the side of the bowl once or twice and gradually adding milk if the mixture seems too stiff.

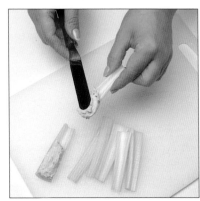

2 If you like, peel the celery lightly to remove any heavy strings before cutting each stalk into 3- to 4-inch pieces. Using a small knife, fill each celery stick with a little cheese mixture and press on a few chopped nuts. Arrange on a serving plate and refrigerate until ready to serve.

COOK'S TIP

For a more elegant presentation, fill a pastry bag fitted with a small star tip with the cheese mixture and carefully pipe mixture into the celery sticks. Press on the nuts.

Italian-style Marinated Artichokes

Good-quality extra-virgin olive oil together with fresh herbs, turn canned or frozen artichoke hearts into a delicious snack.

Makes about 3 cups

INGREDIENTS
2 × 14-ounce cans artichoke hearts
    in salt water
¾ cup extra-virgin olive oil
1 teaspoon chopped fresh thyme, or
    ½ teaspoon dried thyme
1 teaspoon chopped fresh oregano or
    marjoram, or ½ teaspoon dried
    oregano or marjoram
½ teaspoon fennel seeds, lightly
    crushed
1 to 2 garlic cloves, finely chopped
freshly ground black pepper
grated peel and juice of ½ lemon

I Rinse the artichokes, then drain them on paper towels. Cut any large ones in half lengthwise.

thyme

*artichoke
hearts*

lemon

black pepper

oregano

*extra-virgin
olive oil*

lemon peel

fennel seeds

2 Put the artichokes in a large saucepan with the next six ingredients, stir to combine, then cook, covered, over very low heat for 8 to 10 minutes until the flavors infuse. Remove from the heat and leave to cool slightly, then gently stir in the lemon peel and juice. Refrigerate. Return to room temperature before serving on toothpicks.

Prosciutto Grissini

This is an easy way to combine two well-loved ingredients for a quick nibble with no real cooking.

Makes about 24

INGREDIENTS
8 ounces prosciutto, very thinly sliced
1 × 4-ounce box grissini (Italian bread sticks)
basil leaves, to garnish (optional)

grissini

basil leaves

prosciutto

1 If the prosciutto slices are large, lay each slice flat on a board and cut in half lengthwise.

2 Wrap each bread stick with a half-slice of prosciutto, tucking in a basil leaf if you like, to come half way down the bread stick. Arrange on a plate and cover until ready to serve. Garnish with fresh basil if you like.

COOK'S TIP

Do not prepare too far in advance as the moisture from the ham will cause the bread sticks to bend.

VARIATION

Substitute half slices of thinly smoked salmon and garnish with sprigs of dill instead of basil.

Aromatic Greek Olives with Feta

Prepare lots of these and store them in the refrigerator for unexpected guests. They will keep for about a month in a tightly closed container, but remember to bring them to room temperature before serving.

Makes 3 cups

INGREDIENTS
¾ cup virgin olive oil
1 tablespoon cumin seeds, lightly crushed
1 tablespoon coriander seeds, lightly crushed
1 tablespoon fennel seeds, lightly crushed
1 teaspoon cardamom pods, crushed
½ teaspoon crushed red-pepper flakes
¼ teaspoon ground cinnamon
4 to 6 garlic cloves, crushed
grated peel and juice of 1 lemon
3 cups kalamata or other oil-cured olives, drained

TO SERVE
8 ounces feta cheese, cut into ½-inch cubes
1 to 2 tablespoons virgin olive oil
freshly ground black pepper
1 to 2 tablespoons chopped fresh cilantro or parsley

lemon

feta cheese   *kalamata olives*

olive oil

lemon peel

cilantro

coriander seeds

cardamom pods

garlic cloves

red-pepper flakes   *cinnamon*

fennel seeds

1 In a medium-size saucepan, combine the olive oil, spices, and garlic. Cook over medium-low heat for 3 to 5 minutes until warm and fragrant, stirring occasionally.

COOK'S TIP
The seasoned feta cheese cubes make
a delicious nibble on their own.

2 Remove the pan from the heat and
stir in the lemon peel and juice, then add
the olives, tossing until well combined, set
aside to cool. Transfer to an airtight
container or jar to refrigerate.

3 Bring the olives to room
temperature, pour in to a bowl. Put the
feta cubes in another bowl, drizzle the
olive oil over, and season with black
pepper, then sprinkle with chopped
cilantro or parsley. Serve the olives with
the cheese cubes.

Parmesan Phyllo Triangles

You can whip up these light and crunchy triangles at the last minute using fresh or frozen sheets of phyllo pastry.

Makes about 24

INGREDIENTS
3 large sheets phyllo pastry
olive oil, for brushing
3 to 4 tablespoons freshly grated
    Parmesan cheese
½ teaspoon crumbled dried thyme or
    sage

Parmesan cheese

olive oil

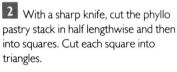

phyllo pastry

1 Preheat the oven to 350°F. Line a large cookie sheet with foil and brush lightly with oil. Lay one sheet of phyllo pastry on a counter and brush lightly with a little olive oil. Sprinkle lightly with half the Parmesan and a little dried thyme or sage. Cover with a second sheet of phyllo, brush with a little more oil, and sprinkle with the remaining cheese and thyme or sage. Top with the remaining sheets of phyllo and brush very lightly with a little more oil.

2 With a sharp knife, cut the phyllo pastry stack in half lengthwise and then into squares. Cut each square into triangles.

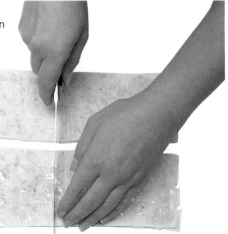

3 Arrange the triangles on the cookie sheet, scrunching them slightly. Do not allow them to touch. Bake for 6 to 8 minutes until crisp and golden. Cool slightly and serve.

COOK'S TIP
These will keep in an airtight container for up to three days, but handle carefully as they are very fragile. Reheat in a medium oven to crisp when you are ready to serve them.

Mini Macaroons

Try these chewy macaroons with a glass of wine —in France, sweet cookies are often served with Champagne.

Makes about 34

INGREDIENTS
1¼ cups blanched almonds
⅔ cup + 1 tablespoon sugar
2 egg whites
½ teaspoon almond or natural vanilla
   extract
confectioners' sugar, for dusting
   (optional)

egg white

sugar

almond extract

blanched almonds

1 Preheat the oven to 400°F. Line a large cookie sheet with nonstick parchment paper. Put the almonds and sugar in the bowl of a food processor and process until very finely ground. With the machine running, slowly add the egg whites. (You may not need all of them; the dough should be soft but hold its shape.) If the mixture is too stiff, add a little more egg white. Carefully mix in the almond or vanilla extract.

2 With moistened hands, shape the mixture into about 34 small balls and arrange on the cookie sheet about 1½ inches apart. With the back of a wet spoon, flatten the tops and dust them lightly with confectioners' sugar.

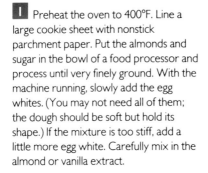

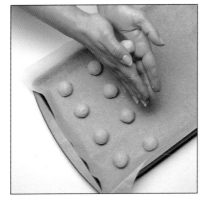

VARIATION

If you like, press an extra blanched almond half on top of each macaroon before baking.

3 Bake for 12 to 15 minutes until the tops just begin to color and the macaroons feel slightly firm. Transfer the cookie sheet to a wire rack to cool, dust with more confectioners' sugar if you like, then remove the macaroons from the paper.

Crudités and Dips

Dips and their accompanying raw vegetables—crudités—seem to be an inevitable feature of any informal gathering, because they are such ideal party food. Just about anything can be included in the crudité category—asparagus spears, zucchini, other raw or blanched vegetables, strips of cheese, melon, cooked chicken . . . all these can be dipped into a variety of mixtures that come from around the world —guacamole from Mexico, hummus and taramasalata from Greece, sweet mustard sauce from Sweden, spicy dhal from India, olivada from Spain, or tapenade from France. The following two dips are easy to make and can be prepared at the last minute.

Slicing Peppers

1 Cut off the bottom of the pepper and stand the pepper on the cut edge. Cut down each side of the core to obtain 4 flat sides.

2 Cut each side into triangular-shaped spears to serve as crudités.

Easy Oriental Dip

Makes about 1 cup

INGREDIENTS
½ cup sunflower oil
¼ cup toasted sesame oil
1-inch piece fresh gingerroot, peeled
1 to 2 garlic cloves, crushed
2 green onions, finely chopped
1 small red chili, seeds removed, finely chopped

sesame oil

green onions

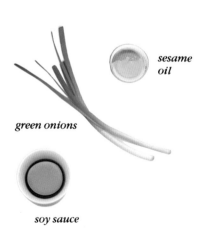

soy sauce

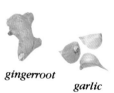

gingerroot   *garlic*   *sunflower oil*

1 Heat the oils in a small saucepan over low heat. Cut the peeled gingerroot into thin slices. Stack the slices and cut into long, thin julienne strips.

2 Turn the strips and cut crosswise into very small dice. Put the diced ginger, garlic, green onions, and chili into the oil and heat for 5 to 7 minutes, to allow the flavors to infuse. Cool and pour into a small bowl and serve with crudités.

VARIATION

Make a sour cream and herb dip by mixing together 1 cup sour cream, 2 finely chopped green onions, and sprigs of fresh herbs such as dill, parsley, and chives. Season with black pepper. You can also add crushed garlic to this dip.

Slicing Fennel

1 Trim the tops and root end of the fennel bulb. If you like, remove the triangular core and cut the bulb in half lengthwise.

2 Cut each half into long strips to serve as crudités.

Tortelloni Kebabs

This hors d'oeuvres is easy to make, and always popular. Any favorite dipping sauce can be substituted, or just drizzle the kebabs with good virgin olive oil and sprinkle with freshly grated Parmesan.

Makes about 64

INGREDIENTS
1 pound fresh cheese-filled tortelloni
2 teaspoons olive oil
basil leaves, to garnish

FOR THE SAUCE
1 × 16-ounce jar roasted red peppers, drained
1 garlic clove, chopped
1 tablespoon olive oil
1 tablespoon balsamic vinegar
1 teaspoon sugar
freshly ground black pepper
2 to 3 dashes hot-pepper sauce

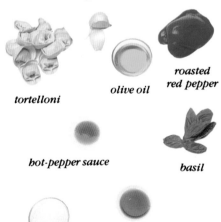

garlic

roasted red pepper

olive oil

tortelloni

hot-pepper sauce

basil

sugar

balsamic vinegar

1 Put the ingredients for the sauce into the bowl of a food processor and process until smooth, scraping down the sides once or twice. Strain into a serving bowl and cover until ready to serve.

2 Bring a large saucepan of lightly salted water to a fast boil. Add the tortelloni and cook according to the directions on the package, 8 to 10 minutes. Drain, rinse in warm water and turn into a bowl. Toss with olive oil to prevent sticking. Cover until ready to serve.

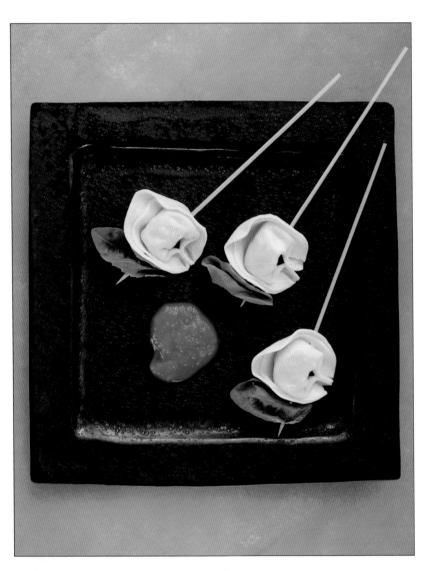

3 Use small, 6-inch wooden skewers, and thread a basil leaf and 1 tortelloni onto each skewer. Arrange on a plate and serve warm, or at room temperature with the dipping sauce.

COOK'S TIP

The sauce can be made up to a day in advance or frozen for several weeks.

Hot Corned Beef on a Stick

This quick nibble on a stick is based on the classic New York delicatessen sandwich, pastrami on rye.

Makes 24

INGREDIENTS
vegetable oil for frying
unsliced rye bread with caraway
 seeds, cut into twenty-four ½-inch
 cubes
8 ounces corned beef or pastrami, in
 one piece
mild mustard for spreading
2 pickled cucumbers, cut into
 small pieces
24 cocktail onions

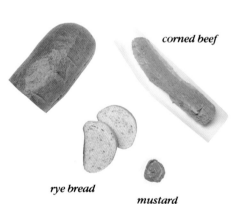

corned beef

rye bread

mustard

cocktail onions

pickled cucumbers

1 In a heavy-bottomed, medium-size skillet, heat ½ inch of oil. When very hot but not smoking add half the bread cubes and fry for about 1 minute until just golden, turning occasionally. Remove with a slotted spoon and drain on a paper towels. Repeat with the remaining cubes.

2 Cut the corned beef or pastrami into ½-inch cubes and spread one side of each cube with a little mustard.

3 Thread a bread cube onto a skewer, then add a piece of meat with the mustard side against the bread, then a piece of pickled cucumber, and finally an onion. Arrange the skewers on a plate or tray, and serve immediately.

Medjol Dates Stuffed with Cream Cheese

These soft, plump fresh dates make an ideal snack. They are available in most large supermarkets.

Makes 24

INGREDIENTS
24 fresh medjol dates
8 ounces cream cheese, softened
grated peel and juice of ½ orange
1 to 2 tablespoons Amaretto liqueur (optional)
½ cup toasted almonds, coarsely chopped

orange

orange peel

medjol dates

toasted almonds

cream cheese

1 With a small sharp knife, split each date lengthwise and remove the pit. In a small bowl, beat the cream cheese with the orange peel and 2 to 3 tablespoons of the juice. Stir in the Amaretto, if using.

2 Spoon the mixture into a small pastry bag fitted with a medium star or plain tip. Pipe a line of filling into each date, then sprinkle with the nuts.

VARIATION
You can use small dates but they are stickier and more fiddly to prepare.

Hot Crab Dip

This delicious creamy dip with a golden almond crust is served hot, with raw vegetables or crackers.

Makes about 2½ cups

INGREDIENTS
8 ounces cream cheese, at room temperature
2 t– 3 tablespoons milk
1 tablespoon brandy or vermouth
2 green onions, finely chopped
1 to 2 teaspoons Dijon mustard
salt
2 to 3 dashes hot-pepper sauce
1 tablespoon chopped fresh dill or parsley
8 ounces white crabmeat, picked over
3 to 4 tablespoons slivered almonds

crabmeat

green onions

cream cheese

dill

Dijon mustard

slivered almonds

vermouth

hot-pepper sauce

1 Preheat the oven to 375°F. In a bowl, using a wooden spoon, beat the cream cheese with all the other ingredients, except the almonds.

2 Spoon the mixture into a small gratin or baking dish and sprinkle with the almonds. Bake for 12 to 15 minutes until the top is golden and the crab mixture hot and bubbling. Serve immediately with a selection of raw vegetables or crackers.

Mini Baked Potatoes with Sour Cream and Chives

Baked potatoes are always delicious, and the toppings can easily be varied—from caviar and smoked salmon to cheese and baked beans.

Makes 36

INGREDIENTS

36 potatoes, about 1½ inches in diameter, well scrubbed
1 cup thick sour cream
3 to 4 tablespoons snipped fresh chives
Kosher salt, for sprinkling

potatoes

sour cream

chives

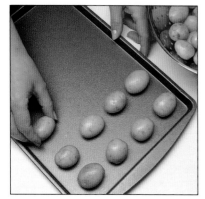

1 Preheat the oven to 350°F. Place potatoes on a baking tray and bake for 30 to 35 minutes, or until tender when pierced with the tip of a knife.

2 To serve, make a cut in the top of each potato and squeeze gently to open. Using the handle of a wooden spoon, make a hole in the center of each potato. Fill each hole with a little sour cream, then sprinkle with the salt and the chives. Serve immediately, or at room temperature.

VARIATION

If your guests are likely to be hungry, use medium-size potatoes. When cooked, cut in half, scoop out the flesh, mash with the other ingredients and spoon the mixture back into the skins. Serve warm.

COOK'S TIP

The potatoes can be baked in advance, then reheated in the microwave on High (100%) for 3 to 4 minutes.

Cheese Balls

These colorful little cheese balls are made in four different flavors, each variety coated with a different herb or seed.

Makes about 48

INGREDIENTS
2 cups cream cheese at room
   temperature
¼ cup grated sharp Cheddar cheese
½ teaspoon dry mustard powder,
   prepared
1 teaspoon mango chutney, chopped
   (optional)
cayenne pepper
salt
2 ounces Roquefort or Stilton cheese
1 tablespoon finely chopped green
   onions or snipped fresh chives
1 to 2 teaspoons bottled pesto sauce
1 tablespoon chopped pine nuts
1 to 2 garlic cloves, finely chopped
2 tablespoons chopped mixed fresh
   herbs, such as parsley, tarragon,
   chives, dill, or cilantro

TO COAT
2 tablespoons paprika
2 tablespoons finely chopped fresh
   parsley
2 tablespoons toasted sesame seeds
coarsely ground black pepper mixed
   with poppy seeds

1 Divide the cream cheese equally between 4 small bowls. Into one mix the Cheddar cheese, mustard, and mango chutney, if using. Season with cayenne pepper and a little salt. Into the second bowl, mix the Roquefort or Stilton cheese and green onions or chives and season with a little cayenne.

2 Mix the pesto sauce and pine nuts into the third bowl and season with a little cayenne. Mix the chopped garlic and mixed fresh herbs into the last bowl of cream cheese. Cover and refrigerate all 4 bowls for about 30 minutes until the cheese is firm enough to handle. Roll each of the different cheese mixtures into small balls, keeping them separate.

3 Lightly dust the Cheddar-flavored balls with paprika, rolling to cover completely. Roll the pesto balls in chopped parsley and the Roquefort balls in sesame seeds. Roll the garlic-herb cheese balls in coarsely ground black pepper and poppy seeds. Arrange the balls on leaves, a plate, or in a lined basket and serve with toothpicks.

green
onions

Cheddar
cheese

garlic

parsley

sesame seeds

cream
cheese

poppy
seeds

dry mustard

pesto sauce

black
pepper

Roquefort cheese

paprika

cayenne
pepper

chopped
pine nuts

mango
chutney

Crostini with Three Vegetable Toppings

This popular Italian hors d'oeuvre was originally a way of using up leftovers, such as ham, cheese, and pâté.

Makes 24

INGREDIENTS
1 ciabatta or French stick

FOR THE ONION-AND-BLACK-OLIVE
  TOPPING
1 tablespoon olive oil
2 red onions, thinly sliced
1 teaspoon sugar
½ teaspoon dried thyme
16 kalamata or other oil-cured ripe
  olives, pitted and halved
bottled tapenade for spreading
  (optional)
parsley leaves, to garnish

FOR THE PEPPER-AND-ANCHOVY
  TOPPING
1 × 14 ounce jar Italian roasted red
  peppers
2 ounces anchovy fillets
extra-virgin olive oil for drizzling
1 to 2 tablespoons balsamic vinegar
1 garlic clove, peeled
2 tablespoons snipped fresh chives,
  oregano, or sage, to garnish
1 tablespoon capers, to garnish

FOR THE MOZZARELLA-AND-TOMATO
  TOPPING
pesto sauce for brushing
½ cup thick homemade or bottled
  tomato sauce or pizza topping
4 ounces good quality mozzarella
  cheese, cut into 8 thin slices
2 or 3 ripe plum tomatoes, seeded and
  cut into strips
fresh basil leaves, to garnish

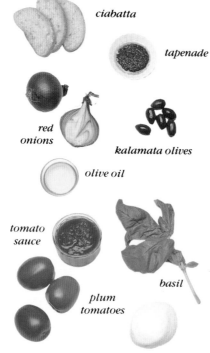

ciabatta

tapenade

red onions

kalamata olives

olive oil

tomato sauce

basil

plum tomatoes

mozzarella cheese

anchovy fillets

balsamic vinegar

chives

capers

garlic cloves

roasted red peppers

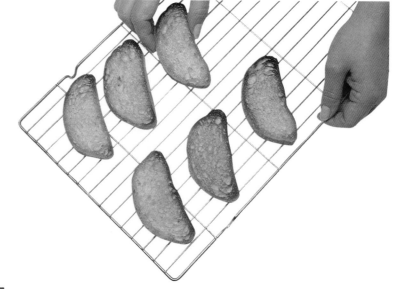

1 Cut the ciabatta or French bread into 24 slices, ½ inch thick. Toast until crisp and golden on both sides. Cool on a wire rack.

2 Prepare the Onion-and-Ripe-Olive Topping. In a heavy-bottomed skillet, heat the olive oil over medium heat and add the onions. Cook slowly for 7 to 10 minutes, stirring frequently, until soft and just beginning to color. Stir in the sugar, thyme, and olives, then remove from the heat to cool. Spread 8 of the toasts with a little tapenade and top with a generous spoonful of the onion mixture. Garnish with parsley.

3 For the Pepper-and-Anchovy Topping, drain the peppers and wipe dry. Cut into ½ inch strips and place in a shallow dish. Rinse and dry the anchovy fillets and add to the peppers. Drizzle with olive oil and sprinkle with the vinegar. Rub 8 toasts with the garlic clove. Arrange the peppers and anchovies on the toasts and sprinkle with herbs and capers. For the Mozzarella-and-Tomato Topping, brush the remaining 8 toasts with pesto sauce and spoon tomato sauce onto each. Arrange a slice of mozzarella cheese on each and cover with the tomato strips. Garnish with basil.

Broiled Brie with Walnuts

This unusual cheese snack looks impressive but requires almost no preparation.

Serves about 16–20

INGREDIENTS
1½ pound wheel of Brie or
   Camembert cheese
1 tablespoon butter, at room
   temperature
1 teaspoon Dijon mustard
¼ cup chopped walnuts
French stick, sliced and toasted,
   to serve

Dijon mustard

Brie wheel

walnuts

butter

Preheat the broiler. In a small bowl, cream together the butter and mustard, and spread evenly over the surface of the cheese. Transfer to a flameproof serving plate, then broil 4 to 6 inches from the heat, for 3 to 4 minutes until the top just begins to bubble.

2 Sprinkle the surface with the walnuts and broil for 2 to 3 minutes longer until the nuts are golden. Serve immediately with the French bread toasts. Allow your guests to help themselves as the whole brie makes an attractive centerpiece.

Spicy Baked Potato Boats

These tasty spiced potato wedges are easy to make, and disappear so quickly it's a good idea to double the recipe!

Makes about 38 wedges

INGREDIENTS
4 medium-size waxy potatoes,
   scrubbed and unpeeled
1 garlic clove, crushed
1 tablespoon cumin seeds
½ teaspoon ground cilantro
½ teaspoon ground black pepper
⅓ cup virgin olive oil
salt

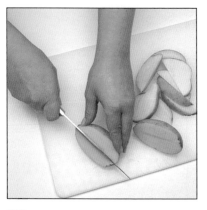

garlic

cilantro

potatoes

olive oil

cumin seeds

black pepper

Preheat the oven to 400°F. Cut the potatoes into boat-shaped wedges about ¾ inch thick. Place in a large bowl and sprinkle with the cumin garlic, cilantro, black pepper, and olive oil and toss to coat well.

2 Lightly grease a large baking tray (preferably nonstick) and warm in the oven. Arrange the potatoes on baking tray in a single layer. Bake for 30 to 35 minutes until tender and golden brown. Sprinkle with salt and serve hot.

Tiny Cheese Puffs

These bite-sized portions of choux pastry are the ideal accompaniment to a glass of wine.

Makes about 45

INGREDIENTS
1 cup all-purpose flour
½ teaspoon salt
1 teaspoon dry mustard powder
pinch cayenne pepper
1 cup water
½ cup butter, cut into pieces
4 eggs
¾ cup finely diced Gruyère cheese
1 tablespoon chives, finely chopped

all-purpose flour

eggs

butter

cayenne pepper

Gruyère cheese

dry mustard powder

1 Preheat the oven to 400°F. Lightly grease 2 large baking trays. Sift together the flour, salt, dry mustard, and cayenne pepper.

2 In a medium-size saucepan, bring the water and butter to a boil over medium-high heat. Remove the pan from the heat and add the flour mixture all at once, beating with a wooden spoon until the dough forms a ball. Return to the heat and beat constantly for 1 to 2 minutes to dry out. Remove from the heat and cool for 3 to 5 minutes.

3 Beat 3 of the eggs in to the dough, one at a time, beating well after each addition. Beat the fourth egg in a small bowl and add a teaspoon at a time beating until the dough is smooth and shiny and falls slowly when dropped from a spoon. (You may not need all the fourth egg; reserve any remaining egg for glazing.) Stir in the diced cheese and chives.

4 Using 2 teaspoons, drop small mounds of dough 2 inches apart on to the baking trays. Beat the reserved egg with 1 tablespoon water and brush the tops with the glaze. Bake for 8 minutes, then reduce the oven temperature to 350°F and bake for 7 to 8 minutes longer until puffed and golden. Remove to a wire rack to cool. Serve warm.

VARIATION

For Ham and Cheese Puffs, add ½ cup finely diced cooked ham with the cheese. For Cheesy Herb Puffs, stir in 2 tablespoons chopped fresh herbs or green onions with the cheese.

COOK'S TIP

The puffs can be prepared ahead and frozen. Reheat in a hot oven for 5 minutes, until crisp, before serving.

Straw Potato Cakes with Caramelized Apple

These little potato cakes resemble *latkes*, a Central European specialty. You must work quickly, because the uncooked potato darkens very rapidly.

Makes about 16

INGREDIENTS
1 tablespoon butter
1 to 2 eating apples, unpeeled, cored and diced
1 teaspoon lemon juice
2 teaspoons sugar
pinch cinnamon
¼ cup thick sour cream

FOR THE POTATO CAKES
oil for frying
½ small onion, very finely chopped or grated
2 baking potatoes
salt
freshly ground black pepper
flat-leaf parsley, to garnish

potatoes
onion
lemon
eating apples
sugar
oil
butter
cinnamon
black pepper

COOK'S TIP
Potato cakes can be prepared in advance and warmed in a preheated 400°F oven for about 5 to 7 minutes, until heated through.

VARIATION
Omit the caramelized apple and top each cake with a few slices of smoked salmon, sprinkled with snipped chives.

1 In a medium-size skillet, melt the butter over medium heat. Add the diced apple and toss to coat. Sprinkle with the lemon juice, sugar, and cinnamon, then cook for 2 to 3 minutes, stirring frequently, until the apples are just tender and beginning to color. Turn into a bowl.

2 Put the grated onion into a bowl. Using a hand or box grater, grate the potatoes onto a clean dish towel and squeeze the potato as dry as possible.

3 Shake into the bowl with the onion and season with the salt and pepper.

4 In a large, heavy-bottomed skillet, heat ½-inch oil, until hot but not smoking. Drop tablespoonfuls of the potato mixture into the oil in batches.

5 Flatten slightly and fry for 5 to 6 minutes. Drain on paper towels. Keep warm. To serve, top each potato cake with 1 teaspoon caramelized apple and then a little sour cream on top. Garnish with flat-leaf parsley.

Angels and Devils on Horseback

The combination of bacon with scallops and chicken livers is surprisingly good. Prepare these in advance, then cook them at the last minute.

Makes 24

INGREDIENTS
12 bacon slices, rind removed
12 scallops, muscle extracted, rinsed
    and dried
12 small chicken livers, gristle and fat
    removed, dried on paper towels
salt and freshly ground black pepper
paprika
1 to 2 tablespoons chopped fresh
    parsley

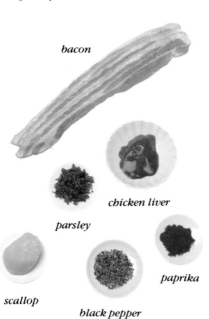

bacon

chicken liver

parsley

paprika

scallop

black pepper

1 Preheat the oven to 450°F. Line a large cookie sheet with foil. Cut the bacon slices in half crosswise and lay them on a counter. Run the back of a large knife blade firmly along each slice to flatten and stretch the bacon.

2 Place a scallop on each slice and season with salt, pepper, and paprika. Sprinkle with a little parsley. Place a chicken liver on the remaining rashers and season. Roll the scallops and livers up in the bacon and secure with toothpicks.

3 Arrange the bacon rolls on the cookie sheet and cook for 8 to 10 minutes until the bacon is crisp and brown and the scallops and livers are just firm to the touch. Serve warm or at room temperature.

VARIATION
Fresh dates stuffed with almonds can be used instead of chicken livers.

Guacamole-filled Cherry Tomatoes

Cherry tomatoes are just the right size for an easy nibble; look for the yellow variety in season. You can make the filling as mild or as spicy as you like.

Makes 24

INGREDIENTS
24 cherry tomatoes
salt
1 large ripe avocado, halved and seed removed
⅓ cup cream cheese
3 to 4 dashes hot-pepper sauce, or to taste
grated peel and juice of ½ lime
1 to 2 tablespoons chopped fresh flat-leaf parsley or cilantro

avocado

lime

pepper sauce

cream cheese

cherry tomatoes

cilantro

1 Turn the tomatoes on to their sides on a chopping board. With a small sharp knife, cut a slice from the bottom of each tomato. Using the handle of a small spoon, scoop out the seeds and sprinkle the cavities with salt. Turn the tomatoes over and drain on paper towels for at least 30 minutes.

2 Scoop out the flesh of the avocado into the bowl of a food processor and add the cream cheese. Process until very smooth, scraping down the sides of the bowl once or twice. Season with salt, hot-pepper sauce, and the lime peel and juice. Add half the chopped parsley or cilantro and process to blend.

COOK'S TIP
The tomatoes can be prepared the day before and stored, covered, in the refrigerator, ready for filling.

3 Spoon the mixture into a pastry bag fitted with a medium star tip and pipe swirls into the tomatoes. Sprinkle with the remaining parsley or cilantro.

Egg and Bacon on Fried Bread

These miniature "English breakfasts" are an amusing way to serve eggs and bacon as party food.

Makes 12

INGREDIENTS
olive or other vegetable oil for frying
3 or 4 slices white bread
3 slices bacon, diced or sliced
12 quail eggs
cherry tomatoes and flat-leaf parsley,
   to garnish

bacon

olive oil

quail eggs

white bread

COOK'S TIP

The bread and bacon can be cooked in advance and kept warm or reheated in the oven when ready to serve, but the eggs should not be cooked more than 30 minutes before serving.

1 Preheat the oven to 300°F. Heat about ½-inch oil in a heavy, medium-size skillet. Use a 2-inch round cookie cutter to cut 12 circles from the bread slices.

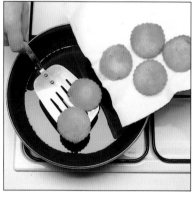

2 When the oil is hot, but not smoking, add the bread circles and fry for 2 to 3 minutes until golden, turning once. Drain on paper towels. You may need to fry the bread in batches. Arrange the bread circles on a baking tray in a single layer.

3 Pour off all but 1 tablespoon oil and add the bacon pieces. Fry for 3 to 5 minutes until crisp and golden. Drain well on paper towels, then put a few bacon pieces on each fried bread circle.

4 Wipe out the pan and add 2 tablespoons fresh oil to the pan. Break in 4 of the quail eggs and cook for 2 to 3 minutes until set. Carefully remove each egg and set on top of the bacon. Continue cooking the eggs in batches, adding a little more oil if necessary, until all are cooked and arranged on the bread circles.

5 Keep the eggs warm in the preheated oven until ready to serve. Cut the cherry tomatoes into quarters. Just before serving arrange the egg-topped bread on a serving dish and garnish each with a cherry tomato quarter and parsley leaf.

VARIATION

If you prefer, instead of frying the eggs, hard-boil them by cooking in boiling water for 2 to 3 minutes. Rinse under cold water and peel. Cut each egg in half and place on the bacon-topped fried bread. Garnish with a piece of chive or a parsley leaf.

Herb-Stuffed Mini Vegetables

These little hors d'oeuvres are ideal for making in advance and assembling and baking at the last minute.

VARIATION
If you wish, after the first 10 minutes of baking remove from the oven, sprinkle the vegetables with grated parmesan, and broil for 3 minutes.

Makes 30

INGREDIENTS
30 mini vegetables, such as zucchini, pattypan squashes, large button mushrooms
fresh basil or parsley, to garnish

FOR THE STUFFING
2 tablespoons olive oil
1 onion, finely chopped
1 garlic clove, finely chopped
1½ cups finely chopped button mushrooms
1 zucchini, finely chopped
1 red pepper, finely chopped
salt and freshly ground black pepper
⅓ cup orzo pasta or long-grain rice
⅓ cup Italian passata (puréed and strained tomatoes)
½ teaspoon dried thyme
½ cup chicken stock
1 to 2 teaspoon chopped fresh basil or parsley
½ cup shredded mozzarella or fontina cheese

1 Prepare the stuffing. In a medium-size skillet or heavy-bottomed saucepan, heat the oil over medium heat. Add the onion and cook for 2 to 3 minutes until just tender. Stir in the garlic, mushrooms, zucchini, and red pepper. Season with salt and pepper and cook for 2 to 3 minutes until the vegetables begin to soften.

2 Stir in the pasta or rice and the passata, then add the thyme and stock and bring to a boil, stirring frequently. Reduce the heat and simmer for 10 to 12 minutes until all the liquid has evaporated and the mixture is thickened. Remove from the heat and cool slightly. Stir in the basil or parsley and cheese and set aside.

3 Prepare the vegetables. Drop the zucchini and pattypan squashes into a large pot of boiling water and cook for 3 minutes. Drain and refresh under cold running water. Trim a thin slice from the length of the zucchini and the bottom of the squashes so they sit firmly on a plate. Trim ¼-inch off the tops and scoop out the centers with a small spoon or melon baller; try not to make any holes in the bottom.

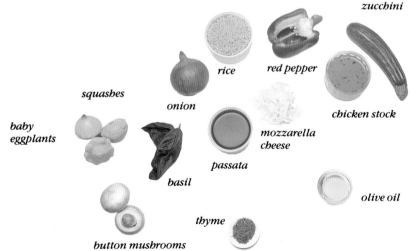

zucchini
rice
red pepper
chicken stock
squashes
onion
mozzarella cheese
baby eggplants
passata
basil
olive oil
thyme
button mushrooms

4 Remove the stems from the center of the mushrooms. If you like, the mushrooms can be blanched like the zucchini or tossed with oil and baked in the oven for 10 minutes at 350°F. Allow to cool before stuffing.

5 Preheat the oven to 350°F. Using a teaspoon carefully fill the prepared vegetables with stuffing. Arrange the vegetables in 2 large baking dishes. Pour in enough boiling water just to cover the bottoms and prevent the vegetables sticking.

6 Cover the dishes tightly with foil and bake for 10 minutes. Uncover and bake for about 5 minutes longer until the fillings are hot and bubbling. Remove from the dish to a wire rack or paper-towel-lined cookie sheet if any water remains. Cool slightly, garnish with basil or parsley and serve warm or at room temperature.

Corn Muffins with Ham

These delicious little muffins are simple to make. If you like, serve them unfilled with a pot of herb butter.

Makes 24

INGREDIENTS

scant ½ cup yellow cornmeal
⅔ cup all-purpose flour
2 tablespoons sugar
1½ teaspoons baking powder
½ teaspoon salt
4 tablespoons butter, melted
½ cup whipping cream
1 egg, beaten
1 or 2 jalapeño or other medium-hot
    chilies, seeded and finely chopped
    (optional)
pinch cayenne pepper
butter for spreading
grainy mustard or mustard with honey
    for spreading
2 ounces oak-smoked ham

whipping cream
all-purpose flour
sugar
grainy mustard
ham
cornmeal
cayenne pepper
baking powder
egg
jalapeño chilies
butter

COOK'S TIP

Muffins can be made in advance and stored in airtight containers. Bring to room temperature or warm slightly before filling and serving.

1 Preheat the oven to 400°F and lightly grease a mini muffin pan with twenty-four 1½-inch cups. In a large bowl, combine the cornmeal, flour, sugar, baking powder, and salt. In another bowl, whisk together the melted butter, cream, beaten egg, chopped chilies, if using, and the cayenne pepper.

2 Make a well in the cornmeal mixture, pour in the egg mixture and gently stir into the dry ingredients just enough to blend (do not overbeat—the batter does not have to be smooth).

3 Drop 1 tablespoon batter into each muffin cup, then bake for 12 to 15 minutes, until golden and just firm to the touch. Remove the pan to a wire rack to cool slightly, then turn out the muffins onto the rack and leave to cool completely.

4 With a sharp knife, split the muffins and spread each bottom half with a little butter and mustard. Cut out small circles of ham with a round cookie cutter, or cut the ham into small squares, and place it on the buttered muffins. Sandwich together each muffin and serve.

Buffalo-Style Chicken Wings

This fiery-hot fried chicken recipe is said to have originated in the town of Buffalo, New York, but is now popular everywhere. Serve it with traditional Blue-cheese Dip and celery sticks.

Makes 48

INGREDIENTS
24 plump chicken wings, tips removed
vegetable oil for frying
salt
6 tablespoons butter
¼ cup hot-pepper sauce, or to taste
1 tablespoon white or cider vinegar
celery sticks, to serve

FOR THE BLUE-CHEESE DIP
4 ounces blue cheese, such as Danish blue
½ cup mayonnaise
½ cup sour cream
2 to 3 green onions, finely chopped
1 garlic clove, finely chopped
1 tablespoon white or cider vinegar

1 To make the dip, use a fork to gently mash the blue cheese against the side of a bowl. Add the mayonnaise, sour cream, green onions, garlic, and vinegar and stir together until well blended. Refrigerate until ready to serve.

green onions

Danish blue cheese

sour cream

vegetable oil

white vinegar

chicken wings

butter

mayonnaise

hot-pepper sauce

2 Using kitchen scissors or a sharp knife, cut each wing in half at the joint to make 48 pieces in all.

3 In a large saucepan or wok, heat 2 inches of oil until hot but not smoking. Fry the chicken wing pieces in small batches for 8 to 10 minutes until crisp and golden, turning once. Drain on paper towels. Season and arrange in a bowl.

4 In a small saucepan over medium-low heat, melt the butter. Stir in the hot-pepper sauce and vinegar and immediately pour over the chicken, tossing to combine. Serve hot with the blue-cheese dip and celery sticks.

Spicy Sun-Dried Tomato Pizza Wedges

These spicy pizza wedges can be made with or without the pepperoni or sausage.

Makes 32

INGREDIENTS

3 to 4 tablespoons olive oil
2 onions, thinly sliced
2 garlic cloves, chopped
8 ounces sliced mushrooms
8 ounces can chopped tomatoes
8 ounces pepperoni or cooked Italian-style spicy sausage, chopped
4 ounces drained and sliced sun-dried tomatoes, packed in oil
1 teaspoon chili flakes
1 teaspoon dried oregano
1 pound bottled marinated artichoke hearts, well drained and cut into quarters
8 ounces shredded mozzarella cheese
4 tablespoons freshly grated Parmesan cheese
fresh basil leaves, to garnish
pitted ripe olives, to garnish

FOR THE DOUGH
1 package pizza-dough mix
cornmeal, for dusting
virgin olive oil for brushing and drizzling

1 Prepare the pizza dough according to the package directions, set aside to rise.

2 Prepare the sauce. In a large, deep skillet, heat the oil over medium-high heat. Add the onions and cook for 3 to 5 minutes until softened. Add the garlic and mushrooms and cook for 3 to 4 minutes more until the mushrooms begin to color.

3 Stir in the chopped tomatoes, pepperoni or sausage, chili flakes, and oregano and simmer for 20 to 30 minutes, stirring frequently, until the sauce is thickened and reduced. Stir in the sun-dried tomatoes, and then set aside to cool slightly.

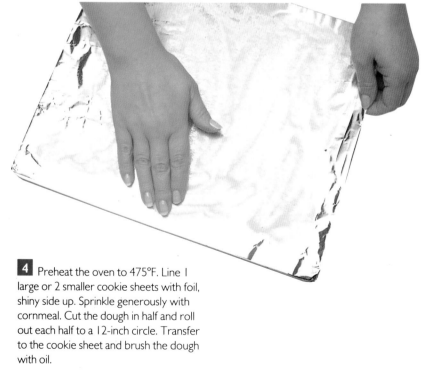

4 Preheat the oven to 475°F. Line 1 large or 2 smaller cookie sheets with foil, shiny side up. Sprinkle generously with cornmeal. Cut the dough in half and roll out each half to a 12-inch circle. Transfer to the cookie sheet and brush the dough with oil.

onion

mushrooms

cornmeal

basil

artichoke hearts

virgin olive oil

pepperoni

ripe olives

oregano

chili flakes

sun-dried tomatoes

grated Parmesan

mozzarella cheese

5 Divide the spicy tomato sauce between the dough circles, spreading to within ½-inch of the edge. Bake for 5 minutes on the lowest shelf of the oven. Arrange half the artichoke hearts over each, sprinkle evenly with the mozzarella and a little Parmesan. Bake each one in the oven on the bottom shelf for 12 to 15 minutes longer, until the edge of the crust is crisp and brown and the topping is golden and bubbling. Remove to a wire rack to cool slightly.

6 Slide the pizzas onto a cutting board and cut each into 16 thin wedges. Garnish each wedge with a ripe olive and basil leaf and serve immediately.

Tortilla Squares

The Spanish tortilla is like the Italian frittata—a flat, baked omelet. Plain or filled, it is always popular.

Makes about 60 squares

INGREDIENTS
4 to 6 tablespoons olive oil, plus extra
   for brushing
1 large onion, thinly sliced
2⅓ cups thinly sliced baking potatoes
2 garlic cloves, finely chopped
½ teaspoon dried thyme
salt and freshly ground black pepper
8 eggs
1 to 2 teaspoons dried oregano or
   basil
¼ teaspoon cayenne pepper or hot-
   pepper sauce, to taste
1 cup frozen peas, thawed and drained
2 to 3 tablespoons freshly grated
   Parmesan cheese
red pepper, to garnish

peas
onion
potatoes
olive oil
egg
garlic clove   Parmesan cheese
cayenne pepper
black pepper   oregano
thyme

COOK'S TIP
If you like, serve a small bowl of chili sauce as a dip for the tortilla squares.

1 In a large, deep, and preferably nonstick, skillet, heat 4 tablespoons of the oil over medium heat. Add the onions and potatoes and cook for 8 to 10 minutes, stirring frequently, until just tender. Add the garlic, thyme, salt, and pepper and cook for 2 minutes longer. Remove from the heat and cool slightly.

2 Preheat the oven to 300°F. Lightly brush an 8- × 12-inch square or 10-inch round baking dish with 2 tablespoons oil. In a mixing bowl, beat the eggs with the oregano or basil, salt, and cayenne pepper until well mixed. Stir in the peas.

3 Spread the cooled potato mixture evenly into the baking dish and carefully pour the beaten egg and pea mixture over. Bake the tortilla for about 40 minutes until just set. Sprinkle with the cheese and bake for 5 minutes longer Remove to a wire rack and cool.

4 Carefully unmold the tortilla, cut into 60 small squares. Serve warm or at room temperature with toothpicks, and garnished with pieces of red pepper.

Monti Cristo Triangles

These opulent little sandwiches are stuffed with ham, cheese, and turkey, dipped in egg, and fried in butter and oil. They are rich and very filling.

Makes 64

INGREDIENTS
16 slices firm-textured, thin-sliced
   white bread
½ cup butter, softened
8 slices oak-smoked ham
3 to 4 tablespoons grainy mustard
8 slices Gruyère or Swiss cheese
3 to 4 tablespoons mayonnaise
8 slices turkey or chicken breast
4 or 5 eggs
¼ cup milk
salt and white pepper
1 teaspoon Dijon mustard
vegetable oil for frying
butter for frying
pimiento-stuffed green olives, to
   garnish
flat-leaf parsley leaves, to garnish

oak-smoked ham

turkey breast *white bread*

butter *grainy mustard* *egg*

Dijon mustard

stuffed olives

Swiss cheese

COOK'S TIP
These sandwiches can be prepared ahead and reheated in a preheated oven at 400°F for 6 to 8 minutes.

1 Arrange 8 of the bread slices on the work surface and spread with half the softened butter. Lay 1 slice of ham on each slice of bread and spread with a little grainy mustard. Cover with a slice of cheese and spread with a little mayonnaise, then cover with a slice of turkey or chicken breast. Butter the remaining bread slices and use to complete the sandwiches. Cut off the crusts, trimming to an even square.

2 In a large, shallow baking dish, beat the eggs, milk, salt and pepper, and Dijon mustard until well combined. Soak the sandwiches in the egg mixture on both sides until the egg has been absorbed.

3 Heat about ½-inch of oil and melted butter in a large, heavy skillet until hot but not smoking. Gently fry the sandwiches in batches for 4 to 5 minutes until crisp and golden, turning them once. Add more oil and butter as necessary. Drain on paper towels.

4 Transfer the sandwiches to a cutting board and cut each into 4 triangles, then cut each in half again to make 64 triangles. Thread a parsley leaf and olive onto a toothpick, then stick into each triangle and serve immediately.

French Country Terrine

This versatile terrine can be served in slices, used to fill sandwiches, or cut into small cubes and threaded onto toothpicks with tiny gherkins or onions.

Makes 1 terrine or loaf

INGREDIENTS
1 pound leeks, trimmed, cut in half
   lengthwise and washed
1 tablespoon butter
2 or 3 garlic cloves, finely chopped
2¼ pounds lean pork, well trimmed,
   cut into pieces
5 ounces smoked bacon
1½ teaspoons chopped fresh thyme
   or 1 teaspoon dried thyme
½ teaspoon dried sage
¼ teaspoon grated nutmeg
½ teaspoon quatre épices or ground
   allspice
½ teaspoon salt
1 teaspoon freshly ground black
   pepper
2 bay leaves
cherry tomatoes, to garnish

TO SERVE
French country bread or a French
   stick, sliced and toasted
French grainy mustard
pickled gherkins
Belgian endive leaves

COOK'S TIP
The pork can be ground in a hand grinder if you do not have a food processor. Alternatively, ask your butcher or the assistant at the supermarket meat counter to coarsely grind a piece of pork leg or shoulder.

1 Thinly slice the leeks. In a large, heavy-bottomed saucepan, melt the butter and stir in the leeks. Cook over low heat, covered, for 10 minutes, stirring occasionally. Stir in the garlic and cook for 5 to 7 minutes longer, until the leeks are tender. Remove from the heat to cool.

2 Put the pork pieces in the bowl of a food processor (you may need to work in 2 or 3 batches) and process carefully until coarsely chopped; do not overprocess. Transfer to a large bowl.

3 Reserve 2 or 3 slices of bacon and process the remaining slices. Add to the pork mixture with the leeks, thyme, sage, quatre épices, nutmeg, and salt and pepper. Using a wooden spoon or your hands, mix until well combined.

bacon

pickled gherkins

sage

pork

grainy mustard

quatre épices

leeks

butter

nutmeg

French bread

bay leaf   black pepper

4 Preheat the oven to 350°F. Grease a heavy, nonstick 6¼-cup terrine or bread pan. Drape the reserved bacon slices diagonally across the pan, pressing into the corners. Put the bay leaves down the center of the pan bottom, then spoon in the terrine mixture, pressing it into the sides and corners. Smooth the top of the terrine and then cover with foil.

5 Put the terrine in a roasting pan and pour in enough boiling water to come half way up the sides of the terrine. Bake for 1 ¼ hours. Cool completely. Place a foil-covered piece of board, cut to fit, on top of the terrine. Weigh it down with 2 heavy cans or weights and refrigerate overnight.

6 To serve, loosen the edges of the terrine with a knife and turn out onto a serving dish or cutting board. Scrape off any congealed fat or juices and cut into thin slices. Serve on endive leaves or pieces of toasted French bread, spread with French grainy mustard and garnished with gherkins and cherry tomatoes.

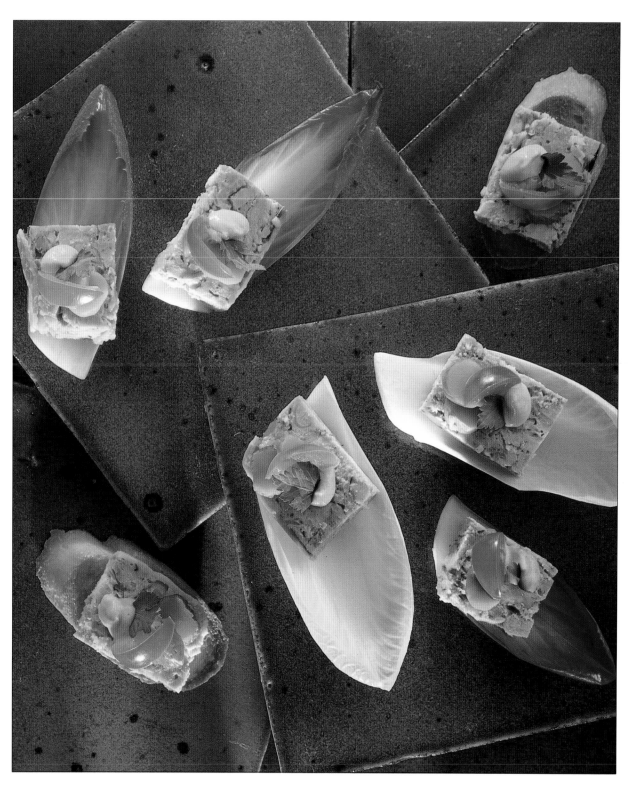

Scandinavian Open-Faced Sandwiches

The Swedes and Danes are famous for their open-faced sandwiches, which are often served as part of a *smörgåsbord*—a huge party buffet of hot and cold dishes.

Makes 16 halves

INGREDIENTS

ROAST BEEF WITH HORSERADISH CREAM

3 to 4 tablespoons mayonnaise
1 tablespoon horseradish sauce
2 to 3 dashes hot-pepper sauce
4 slices rye bread
4 slices very rare tender roast beef
diced sweet-and-sour pickled cucumber
watercress, to garnish

GRAVLAX WITH HONEY-DILL MUSTARD SAUCE

2 to 3 tablespoons mayonnaise
2 teaspoons Dijon mustard
1 tablespoon honey
1 teaspoon vegetable oil
1 tablespoon chopped fresh dill
4 slices whole-wheat bread
4 to 8 slices gravlax (cured salmon), depending on slice size
cucumber slices, to garnish

SMOKED CHICKEN AND AVOCADO WITH LIME

8 ounces smoked chicken breast half, skin removed
1 small ripe avocado, diced
¼ cup garlic mayonnaise
juice of ½ lime
4 slices pumpernickle or black rye bread
1 to 2 teaspoons butter, softened
curly endive leaves, optional
lime slices, to garnish

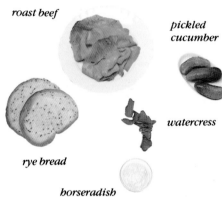
roast beef
pickled cucumber
rye bread
watercress
horseradish sauce

gravlax
avocado

cucumber *dill* *Dijon mustard*
pumpernickle
smoked chicken breast half

COOK'S TIP

All sandwiches are best made immediately before serving. The toppings can be prepared in advance, and then assembled at the last minute.

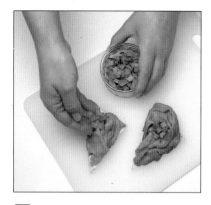

1 To make the Roast Beef with Horseradish, in a small bowl, combine the mayonnaise and horseradish and hot-pepper sauces according to taste. Spread the rye bread slices with the horseradish sauce. Arrange the roast beef in folds for a more attractive appearance on the bread and cut each slice into 2 triangles. Sprinkle each with a little pickled cucumber chopped into cubes and garnish with watercress.

2 For the Gravlax with Honey Dill Mustard, in a small bowl, combine the mayonnaise, mustard, honey, oil, and dill. Reserve 1 to 2 tablespoons for the garnish. Cut each slice of bread into 2 triangles and spread with the horseradish sauce. Arrange the gravlax on each triangle overlapping slightly, and garnish with cucumber slices and the remaining sauce.

3 For the Smoked Chicken and Avocado, slice the chicken. Toss the diced avocado in a bowl with the mayonnaise and lime juice until just blended.

4 Spread the pumpernickle bread slices with a little softened butter and cut each slice into 2 triangles. Arrange a few slices of chicken on the bread and top with a spoonful of the avocado mixture. Garnish with lime slices and a sprig of mint.

Greek Meze with Pita Crisps

Meze are a selection of Greek hors d'oeuvres, and these three dips are quick and easy to make in a food processor. They also go well together—serve them with raw vegetables or these wonderful pita crisps.

INGREDIENTS

FOR THE TZATZIKI (Makes about 3 cups)
2½ cups plain yogurt
1 large cucumber
1 teaspoon salt
1 or 2 garlic cloves, finely chopped
2 or 3 tablespoons chopped fresh mint or 1 tablespoon dried mint
1 or 2 tablespoons virgin olive oil (optional)
mint sprigs, to garnish

FOR THE HUMMUS (Makes about 2½ cups)
heaped 2 cups canned garbanzo beans
3½ tablespoons tahini (sesame paste)
3½ tablespoons freshly squeezed lemon juice
1 to 2 garlic cloves, crushed
salt
cayenne pepper, to taste
1 or 2 tablespoons olive oil
1 or 2 tablespoons chopped fresh parsley or cilantro
olive or sesame oil for drizzling

FOR THE SMOKY EGGPLANT DIP (Makes about 2 cups)
1 large eggplant (about 1 pound)
4 tablespoons freshly squeezed lemon juice
4 tablespoons tahini or mayonnaise
2 or 3 garlic cloves, chopped
salt
2 tablespoons virgin olive oil
2 tablespoons chopped fresh parsley

yogurt

cucumber

mint

olive oil

garbanzo beans

lemon

chopped parsley

cayenne pepper

tahini

eggplant

garlic

FOR THE PITA CRISPS
4 large pita breads
olive oil
dried oregano or *herbes de Provence*
salt

1 To make the Tzatziki, peel the cucumber and cut it lengthwise into quarters. Cut out the seeds, chop finely, and place in a colander. Sprinkle with the salt and leave to drain for about 1 hour.

Pat dry with paper towels. Put the yogurt in a bowl and stir in the drained cucumber, garlic, and mint. Slowly blend in the olive oil, if using. Spoon into a serving bowl, garnish with mint and refrigerate.

2 To make the Hummus, drain the garbanzo beans, reserving the liquid, set aside a few beans for garnishing. Put the remaining beans in a food processor and add the tahini, lemon juice, and garlic. Process until very smooth, scraping down the side of the bowl occasionally. Season with the salt and cayenne pepper and process to blend.

3 With the machine running, slowly pour in 1 to 2 tablespoons olive oil and some of the reserved bean liquid to thin the purée if necessary. Pour into a shallow serving bowl and spread it up the side of the bowl, swirling with the back of a spoon. Pour a little extra olive oil or sesame oil in the center, add the reserved garbanzos, and sprinkle with cayenne pepper. Sprinkle with the chopped parsley or cilantro.

4 To make the Smoky Eggplant Dip, if possible, barbecue the eggplant over a charcoal fire for about 30 minutes. Alternatively, place on a rack with a tray placed below, in the center of a preheated oven, 400°F. Bake for about 30 minutes or until soft, turning, frequently. Remove from the oven. When cool enough to handle, scoop out the flesh into the bowl of a food processor. Add the lemon juice, tahini or mayonnaise, garlic, salt to taste, olive oil, and 1 tablespoons of the parsley. Process for 1 to 2 minutes until very smooth, scraping the sides of the bowl once or twice. Pour into a shallow bowl and garnish with the remaining parsley.

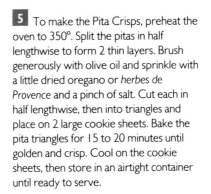

5 To make the Pita Crisps, preheat the oven to 350°. Split the pitas in half lengthwise to form 2 thin layers. Brush generously with olive oil and sprinkle with a little dried oregano or *herbes de Provence* and a pinch of salt. Cut each in half lengthwise, then into triangles and place on 2 large cookie sheets. Bake the pita triangles for 15 to 20 minutes until golden and crisp. Cool on the cookie sheets, then store in an airtight container until ready to serve.

COOK'S TIP

You can, of course, serve these dips with warmed pita bread, but for parties these crisps are ideal because they don't spoil, and they are cooked in advance, so do make the extra effort—it's worth it!

Corn Fritters with Red-Pepper Salsa

The salsa can also be served with grilled chicken or vegetable kebabs. Add the chilies slowly and according to your taste, as they can be very hot.

Makes about 48

INGREDIENTS
corn or other vegetable oil
1 pound frozen or canned corn
    kernels, drained
1 cup all-purpose flour
½ cup yellow cornmeal
1 cup milk
2 teaspoons baking powder
2 teaspoons sugar
1 teaspoon salt
½ teaspoon nutmeg
½ teaspoon cayenne pepper
4 eggs, lightly beaten
cilantro leaves, to garnish

FOR THE SALSA
4 ounces cherry tomatoes, chopped
½ cup frozen or canned corn kernels,
    drained
1 red-pepper, cored and finely
    chopped
½ small red onion, finely chopped
juice of 1 lemon
2 tablespoons olive oil
2 tablespoons chopped fresh cilantro
1 to 2 fresh chilies, seeded and finely
    chopped
salt
½ teaspoon sugar

1 Prepare the salsa at least 2 hours ahead. Combine the ingredients in a bowl, crushing them lightly with the back of a spoon to release the juices. Cover and refrigerate until ready to use.

2 In a bowl, combine 2 tablespoons of the oil with the corn, flour, cornmeal, milk, baking powder, sugar, salt, nutmeg, cayenne pepper, and eggs until just blended; do not overbeat. If the batter is too stiff, stir in a little more milk or water.

3 In a large, heavy-based skillet, heat ½-inch oil until hot but not smoking. Drop tablespoonsful of the batter into the hot oil and cook for 3 to 4 minutes until golden, turning each fritter over once. Drain on paper towels. Arrange on cookie sheets and keep warm for up to 1 hour in an oven at 325°F.

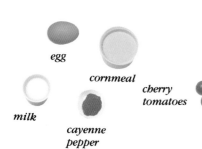

egg

cornmeal

milk

cayenne pepper

cherry tomatoes

lemon

nutmeg

red onion

corn kernels

chili

olive oil

red pepper

chopped cilantro

4 Arrange the corn fritters on a serving plate. Top each with a spoonful of salsa and garnish with a cilantro leaf. Serve hot or warm.

COOK'S TIP
The salsa can be made up to a day in advance. Keep in the refrigerator, covered.

Mini Sausage Rolls

These miniature versions of old-fashioned sausage rolls are always popular—the Parmesan cheese gives them an extra-special flavor.

Makes about 48

VARIATION

Phyllo pastry can be used instead of puff dough for a very light effect. Depending on the size of the phyllo sheets, cut into 8 pieces 10 × 3 inches. Brush 4 of the sheets with a little melted butter or vegetable oil and place a second phyllo sheet on top. Place one sausage log on each of the layered sheets and roll up and bake as below.

INGREDIENTS
1 tablespoon butter
1 onion, finely chopped
12 ounces good-quality sausagemeat
1 tablespoon dried mixed herbs, such as oregano, thyme, sage, tarragon, or dill
salt and pepper
¼ cup finely chopped pistachio nuts (optional)
12 ounces puff pastry dough
4 to 6 tablespoons freshly grated Parmesan cheese
1 egg, lightly beaten, for glazing
poppy seeds, sesame seeds, fennel seeds, or aniseeds for sprinkling

sausagemeat
dried mixed herbs
puff pastry dough
egg
Parmesan cheese
fennel seeds
sesame seeds
pistachio nuts
poppy seeds
onion
butter

1 In a small skillet, over medium heat, melt the butter. Add the onion and cook for about 5 minutes until softened. Remove from the heat and cool. Put the onion, sausagemeat, herbs, salt and pepper, and nuts (if using) in a mixing bowl and stir together until blended.

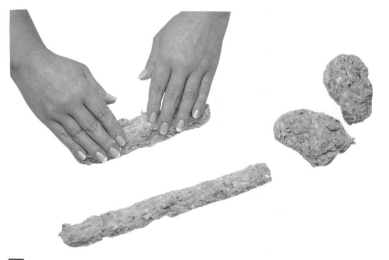

2 Divide the sausage mixture into 4 equal portions, then roll into thin sausages about 10 inches long; set aside.

3 On a lightly floured surface, roll out the dough to about ⅛ inch thick. Cut the pastry into 4 strips 10 × 3 inches long. Place a long sausage on each dough strip and sprinkle each with a little Parmesan cheese.

4 Brush one long edge of each of the dough strips with the egg glaze and roll up to enclose each long sausage. Set them seam-side down and press gently to seal. Brush each with the egg glaze and sprinkle with one type of seeds. Repeat with remaining dough strips and different seeds.

5 Preheat the oven to 425°F. Lightly grease a large cookie sheet. Cut each of the dough rolls into 1 inch pieces and arrange on the cookie sheet. Bake for 15 minutes until the pastry is crisp and brown. Serve warm or at room temperature.

Smoked Trout Mousse in Cucumber Cups

This delicious creamy mousse can be made in advance and kept for 2 or 3 days in the refrigerator. Serve it in crunchy cucumber cups, or simply with crudités.

Makes about 24

INGREDIENTS
½ cup cream cheese, softened
2 green onions, chopped
1 to 2 tablespoons chopped fresh dill
   or parsley
1 teaspoon horseradish sauce
8 ounces smoked trout fillets, flaked
   and any fine bones removed
2 to 4 tablespoons heavy cream
salt
cayenne pepper, to taste
2 cucumbers
dill sprigs, to garnish

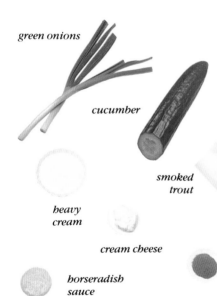

green onions

cucumber

smoked trout

heavy cream

cream cheese

horseradish sauce

cayenne pepper

dill

VARIATION
For Smoked Salmon Mousse, use smoked salmon pieces instead of smoked trout.

1 Put the cream cheese, green onions, dill, and horseradish sauce into the bowl of a food processor and process until well blended. Add the trout and process until smooth, scraping down the side of the bowl once. With the machine running, pour in the cream until a soft mousselike mixture forms. Season, turn into a bowl, and refrigerate for at least 15 minutes.

2 Using a canelle knife or vegetable peeler, score the length of each cucumber to create a striped effect. Cut each cucumber into ¾-inch-thick slices. Using a small spoon or melon baller, scoop out the seeds from the center of each round.

3 Spoon the mousse into a pastry bag fitted with a medium star tip and pipe swirls of the mixture into the cucumber slices. Refrigerate until ready to serve. Garnish each with a small sprig of dill.

Carpaccio Rolls with Anchovy Mayonnaise

This classic hors d'oeuvre of raw beef makes an extravagant but delicious treat.

Makes about 24

INGREDIENTS

8 ounces beef tenderloin, cut from the narrow end and frozen for 1 hour
4 tablespoons virgin olive oil
1 tablespoon lemon juice
freshly ground black pepper
arugula or flat-leaf parsley, to garnish
capers, to garnish
Belgian endive leaves or short celery sticks, to serve

FOR THE ANCHOVY MAYONNAISE

4 to 6 anchovy fillets, drained
1 cup homemade or good quality mayonnaise
1 tablespoon capers, rinsed, drained and chopped
1 small garlic clove, crushed
2 tablespoons freshly grated Parmesan cheese

lemon   Parmesan cheese

beef tenderloin

anchovy fillets

virgin olive oil

mayonnaise

capers   garlic

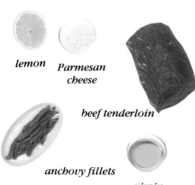

1 To make the Anchovy Mayonnaise, in a bowl, mash the anchovy fillets with a fork, then beat in the mayonnaise, capers, garlic, and Parmesan cheese until well blended.

2 Slice the beef into as many wafer-thin pieces as possible and arrange flat on a cookie sheet. Brush each piece with the olive oil and sprinkle with a little lemon juice and black pepper.

3 Place about ½ a teaspoon Anchovy Mayonnaise in the center of each beef slice, then fold the beef into quarters, or roll it up.

4 To serve, place a rocket leaf at the bottom of an endive leaf and place a rolled or folded up slice of beef on top. Sprinkle with a few capers if you like. If you prefer, skewer each beef parcel with a toothpick and serve on its own.

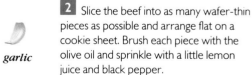

Spicy Crab Cakes

These are miniature versions of a classic New England specialty. Use fresh crabmeat if your budget allows.

Makes about 30

INGREDIENTS
8 ounces crabmeat, drained and
    picked over
1½ cups fresh white bread crumbs
2 green onions, finely chopped
1 to 2 tablespoons chopped fresh dill
    or parsley
1 egg, lightly beaten
¼ cup mayonnaise
1 tablespoon Dijon mustard
1 to 2 tablespoons lemon juice
salt
1 small green chili, seeded and
    chopped (optional)
2 to 3 dashes hot-pepper sauce
fine dried bread crumbs for coating
vegetable oil for frying

FOR THE SEAFOOD COCKTAIL SAUCE
½ cup horseradish sauce
1 to 2 tablespoons mayonnaise
¼ cup tomato ketchup
lemon juice, to taste

crabmeat   bread crumbs

chili

egg   mayonnaise   Dijon
                     mustard

parsley

tomato
ketchup

horseradish
sauce

hot-pepper
sauce

green
onions

lemon

1 To make the Seafood Cocktail Sauce, combine all the ingredients. Refrigerate. For the crab cakes, in a large bowl, combine all the ingredients, except the oil and dried breadcrumbs.

2 Using a small ice-cream scoop or teaspoon, form the mixture into walnut-sized balls. Place on a baking tray.

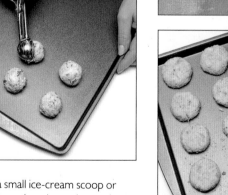

3 Put the dried bread crumbs in a shallow plate and coat the crab balls, a few at a time, rolling to cover completely. Place on a baking tray and flatten each ball slightly until ½ inch thick. Refrigerate for at least 30 minutes.

4 In a large, heavy-bottomed skillet heat ½-inch oil until hot but not smoking. Fry the crab cakes, in batches, for about 2 minutes until crisp and golden, turning once. Serve hot or warm with the sauce.

Smoked Salmon Nests on Wild-Rice Pancakes

The nutty flavor of wild rice provides a perfect foil to the smoky richness of the salmon, in this elegant hors d'oeuvre.

Makes about 24

INGREDIENTS
8 ounces smoked salmon
3 to 4 tablespoons creamed
    horseradish sauce
fresh chives or dill, to garnish

FOR THE WILD-RICE PANCAKES
½ cup all-purpose flour
salt and white pepper
1 egg, lightly beaten
¼ cup milk
1⅓ cups cooked wild-rice
2 tablespoons chopped chives or dill
vegetable oil for frying

vegetable oil

milk

egg

horseradish sauce

all-purpose flour

chives

smoked salmon   *wild-rice*

1 To make the Wild-Rice Pancakes, sift the flour, and salt and pepper into a medium-size bowl and make a well in the center. Put the egg and milk in the well and, using a wire whisk or electric beater on slow speed, gradually bring in the flour from the edges to form a smooth batter. Stir in the wild rice and chives or dill.

VARIATION
The same effect can be achieved more simply by making little bread slices, instead of pancakes. Cut out 2-inch circles from white or whole-wheat sliced bread and toast lightly under a broiler on both sides before adding the topping.

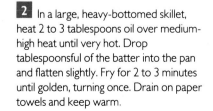

2 In a large, heavy-bottomed skillet, heat 2 to 3 tablespoons oil over medium-high heat until very hot. Drop tablespoonsful of the batter into the pan and flatten slightly. Fry for 2 to 3 minutes until golden, turning once. Drain on paper towels and keep warm.

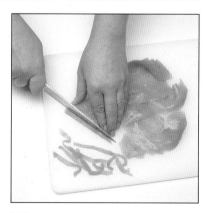

3 With a sharp knife, cut the smoked salmon into thin strips. Spoon a little horseradish cream onto each pancake and top with a pile of salmon strips, twisting to form a nest. If you like, garnish with extra dollops of horseradish cream and fresh chives or dill.

Foie Gras Pâté in Phyllo Cups

This is an extravagantly rich hors d'oeuvre—save it for a special occasion.

Makes about 24

INGREDIENTS
8 ounces canned foie gras pâté or
 other fine liver pâté, at room
 temperature
4 tablespoons butter, softened
2 to 3 tablespoons Cognac or other
 brandy (optional)
3 to 6 sheets fresh or defrosted phyllo
 pastry
3 tablespoons butter, melted
chopped pistachio nuts, to garnish

phyllo pastry

foie gras pâté

pistachio nuts

butter

Cognac

COOK'S TIP
The pâté and pastry are best eaten
soon after preparation. If preparing
ahead and refrigerating, be sure to
bring back to room temperature
before serving.

1 Preheat the oven to 400°F. Grease a muffin pan with twenty-four 1½-inch cups. Stack the phyllo sheets on a work surface and cut into 2½-inch squares. Cover with a damp towel.

2 Keeping the rest of the phyllo squares covered, place one square on the counter and brush lightly with melted butter, then turn and brush the other side. Butter a second square and place it over the first at an angle. Butter a third square and place at an angle over the first 2 sheets to form an uneven edge.

3 Press the layers into the cup of the bun tray. Continue with the remaining pastry and butter until all the cups are filled.

4 Bake the phyllo cups for 4 to 6 minutes until crisp and golden, then remove and cool in the pan for 5 minutes. Carefully remove each phyllo cup to a wire rack and cool completely.

5 In a small bowl, beat the pâté with the softened butter until smooth and well blended. Add the Cognac or brandy to taste, if using. Spoon into a pastry bag fitted with a medium star tip and pipe a swirl into each cup. Sprinkle with pistachio nuts. Refrigerate until ready to serve.

Grilled Asparagus Tips with Easy Hollandaise Sauce

Delicate asparagus tips and buttery rich Hollandaise Sauce make a classic combination and a delicious treat.

Makes 24

INGREDIENTS
24 large asparagus spears
oil for brushing
freshly grated Parmesan cheese for
 sprinkling

FOR THE HOLLANDAISE SAUCE
¾ cup butter, cut into pieces
2 egg yolks
1 tablespoon lemon juice
1 tablespoon water
salt and cayenne pepper

asparagus

egg yolks

butter

cayenne pepper

lemon

COOK'S TIP
Keep the Hollandaise Sauce warm by storing it in a vacuum flask until ready to store.

1 To make the Hollandaise Sauce, melt the butter in a small saucepan and skim off any foam which bubbles to the top.

2 Put the egg yolks, lemon juice, and water into a blender or a food processor. Season with salt and cayenne pepper and blend or process to mix. With the machine running, slowly pour in the hot butter in a thin stream; do not pour in the milky solids on the bottom of the pan.

3 Using a vegetable peeler, peel the asparagus spears. Cut off the stalks to leave tips of about 5 inches. (Reserve the stems for another dish, such as Stir-Fried Vegetable Cups.)

4 Cook the tips in boiling salted water for 2 to 3 minutes until just tender; do not overcook. Refresh under cold water to stop them cooking, then cover until ready to serve.

5 Preheat the broiler. Line a cookie sheet with foil and brush each asparagus tip with a little oil. Sprinkle each tip with a little Parmesan cheese, then broil for 2 to 3 minutes, turning once. Arrange the asparagus on a plate, and serve with the Hollandaise Sauce for dipping.

VARIATION
Wrap each asparagus tip in a thin strip of bacon or prosciutto and brush with oil before broiling. If you like, cut the remainder of the asparagus spears into 3-inch pieces and broil them, for slightly longer, as well.

Marinated Mussels

This is an ideal recipe to prepare and arrange well in advance. Remove from the refrigerator 15 minutes before serving to allow the flavors to develop.

Makes 48

INGREDIENTS

2¼ pounds fresh mussels, large if possible
¾ cup dry white wine
1 garlic clove, well crushed
freshly ground black pepper
½ cup olive oil
¼ cup lemon juice
1 teaspoon hot chili flakes
½ teaspoon apple pie spice
1 tablespoon Dijon mustard
2 teaspoons sugar
1 teaspoon salt
1 to 2 tablespoons chopped fresh dill or cilantro
1 tablespoon capers, diced, drained and chopped if large

lemon　　　*mussels*

sugar

olive oil

mixed spice　　*capers*

garlic

Dijon mustard

dill

hot chili flakes

1 With a stiff kitchen brush, under running cold water, scrub the mussels to remove any sand and barnacles; pull out and remove any beards. Discard any open shells that will not shut when tapped.

3 Meanwhile, in a large bowl, combine the olive oil, lemon juice, chili flakes, apple pie spice, Dijon mustard, sugar, salt, chopped dill or cilantro, and capers.

4 Discard any mussels with closed shells. With a small sharp knife, carefully remove remaining mussels from their shells, reserving 48 shells for serving. Add the mussels to the marinade. Toss the mussels to coat well, then cover and refrigerate for 6 to 8 hours, or overnight, stirring gently from time to time.

COOK'S TIP

Mussels can be prepared ahead and marinated for up to 24 hours. To serve, arrange the mussel shells on a bed of crushed ice, well-washed seaweed, or even kosher salt to stop them wobbling on the plate.

2 In a large flameproof casserole or saucepan over high heat, bring the white wine to a boil with the garlic and freshly ground black pepper. Add the mussels and cover. Reduce the heat to medium and simmer for 2 to 4 minutes until the shells open, stirring occasionally.

5 With a teaspoon, place one mussel with a little marinade in each shell. Arrange on a platter and cover until ready to serve.

A Trio of Tartlets

Tender pastry topped with luscious ingredients always look irresistible—and taste even better! Vary the toppings according to the occasion.

Makes about 24

INGREDIENTS
1⅓ cups all-purpose flour
½ tsp salt
6 tablespoons butter, cut into pieces
1 egg yolk beaten with 2 to 3
    tablespoons cold water

FOR THE SCRAMBLED EGG AND CAVIAR
1 tablespoon butter
2 eggs, lightly beaten
salt and white pepper
1 tablespoon heavy cream or crème
    fraîche
1 to 2 tablespoons caviar or lumpfish
    caviar (optional)

FOR THE SMOKED SALMON AND LEEK
½ cup heavy cream
1 leek, split lengthwise, washed and
    thinly sliced
salt and freshly ground black pepper
pinch of grated nutmeg
4 ounces smoked salmon, sliced very
    thinly
dill sprigs, to garnish

FOR THE ASPARAGUS AND BRIE
1 tablespoon butter
6 asparagus stalks cut into 1½-inch
    pieces
salt
2 ounces Brie, rind removed and
    sliced

flour

salt

caviar

eggs

heavy cream

butter

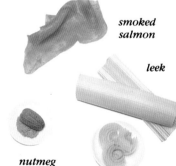
smoked salmon

leek

nutmeg

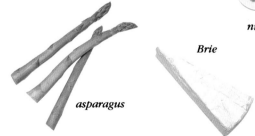
asparagus

Brie

1 To make the dough, put the flour, salt, and butter into the bowl of a food processor and process quickly, until the mixture resembles fine crumbs. Reserve 1 tablespoon of the egg mixture. With the processor running, pour in the remaining egg mixture until the dough just begins to come together (do not allow it to form a ball or it may toughen). If the dough is too dry, add a little more water and process briefly again. Put the dough onto a piece of plastic wrap and use the plastic to push it together and flatten to form a disk shape. Wrap tightly; refrigerate for 1½ hours.

2 On a lightly floured counter, roll out the dough until ⅛ inch thick. Lay out about twelve 2-inch tartlet pans. Lay the dough over the pans and press out. Reroll the trimmings and repeat. Line 24 cases, then prick the bottoms with a fork and refrigerate for 30 minutes.

3 Preheat the oven to 375°F. Put a small piece of crumbled foil into each shell and place on a baking tray. Bake for 6 to 8 minutes until the edges are golden.

Remove the foil and brush each pastry bottom with a little of the reserved egg mixture. Bake for 2 minutes until dry. Transfer to a wire rack to cool.

4 Prepare the fillings: for the Scrambled Egg and Caviar, melt the butter in a small skillet over medium-low heat. Season the eggs with salt and white pepper and add to the pan. Cook the eggs slowly, stirring constantly, until smooth and just set. Remove from the heat and stir in the cream or crème fraîche. Spoon into 8 of the pastry shells. Just before serving, garnish each tartlet with a pinch of caviar. Serve warm or at room temperature.

5 For the Smoked Salmon and Leek filling, bring the cream to a simmer in a pan over medium heat. Add the leeks and cook, stirring frequently, until just tender and the cream is completely reduced. Season with salt, pepper, and a pinch of nutmeg. Spoon into 8 of the pastry shells and top with smoked salmon strips and sprigs of dill just before serving. Serve warm or at room temperature.

6 For the Asparagus and Brie filling, melt the butter in a skillet over medium-high heat. Add the asparagus pieces and stir-fry for 2 to 3 minutes until tender. Divide among the remaining tartlet shells and sprinkle each with a little salt. Divide the Brie among the tartlets. Just before serving, return to the oven for 1 to 2 minutes until the Brie softens. Serve straight away before the cheese hardens.

Cook's Tip

If you do not have 24 tartlet pans, you will need to work in batches. Divide the dough in half or quarters and refrigerate the portion you are not using immediately.

Hazelnut Sablés with Goat Cheese and Strawberries

Sablés are little French cookies, made from egg yolk and butter. Crisp and slightly sweet, they contrast perfectly with the tangy goat cheese and juicy strawberries.

Makes about 24

INGREDIENTS
6 tablespoons butter, at room
   temperature
1 cup all-purpose flour
6 tablespoons blanched hazelnuts,
   lightly toasted and ground
2 tablespoons superfine sugar
2 egg yolks beaten with 2 to 3
   tablespoons water
4 ounces goat cheese
4 to 6 large strawberries, cut into
   small pieces
chopped hazelnuts, to decorate

goat cheese *strawberries*

chopped hazelnuts

ground hazelnuts *butter*

egg yolks

flour

1 To make the dough, put the butter, flour, ground hazelnuts, sugar, and beaten egg yolks into the bowl of a food processor and process until a smooth dough forms.

VARIATION

These sablés are ideal served with fruit. Beat 6 tablespoons cream cheese with 1 tablespoon confectioners' sugar and a little lemon or orange peel. Spread a little on the sablé and top with a few pieces of sliced kiwi fruit, peach, nectarine and a few raspberries or cut-up strawberries.

2 Scrape the dough out onto a sheet of plastic wrap and use the plastic to shape the dough into a log about 1½ inches in diameter. Wrap tightly and refrigerate for 2 hours, or overnight, until very firm.

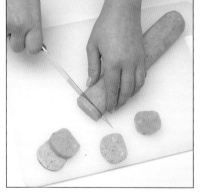

3 Preheat the oven to 400°F and line a large cookie sheet with nonstick parchment paper. With a sharp knife, slice the dough into ¼-inch thick slices and arrange on the cookie sheet. Bake for 7 to 10 minutes until golden brown. Remove to a wire rack to cool and crisp slightly.

4 On a plate, crumble the goat cheese into small pieces. Mound a little goat cheese on to each sablé, top with a piece of strawberry and sprinkle with a few hazelnuts. Serve warm.

Rich Chocolate and Fruit Fondue

This sumptuous fruit fondue, with its rich, delicious sauce, makes a lavish finish to a party.

Makes 1½ cups

INGREDIENTS

a selection of mixed fruit, such as
    kumquats, apple, peach and pear
    slices, banana slices, clementine
    segments, seedless grapes, cherries,
    peeled lychees, mango and papaya
    cubes, cut figs and plums
lemon juice

FOR THE CHOCOLATE FONDUE

8 ounces good-quality semisweet
    chocolate, chopped
2 tablespoons corn syrup
2 tablespoons whipping cream
2 to 3 tablespoons brandy or orange-
    flavored liqueur

peach

clementine   *strawberries*

cherries

fig   *lychees*

plum

kumquat   *grapes*

whipping cream

semisweet chocolate   *brandy*   *lemon juice*

1 Arrange the fruits in an attractive pattern on a large serving dish. Brush any cut-up fruit such as apples, pears, or banana with lemon juice to prevent darkening. Cover and refrigerate until ready to serve.

2 In a medium-size saucepan over medium-low heat, combine the chopped chocolate, corn syrup, and whipping cream. Stir until the chocolate is melted and smooth. Remove from the heat and stir in the brandy or liqueur. Pour into a serving bowl and serve with the chilled fruits and toothpicks.

VARIATION

You can also use small cookies for dipping as well as, or instead of, the pieces of fruit.

Shrimp Toasts

These crunchy sesame-topped toasts are simple to prepare using a food processor for the shrimp paste.

Makes 64

INGREDIENTS
8 ounces cooked, shelled shrimp, well
   drained and dried
1 egg white
2 green onions, chopped
1 teaspoon chopped fresh root ginger
1 garlic clove, chopped
1 teaspoon cornstarch
½ teaspoon salt
½ teaspoon sugar
2 to 3 dashes hot-pepper sauce
8 slices firm-textured white bread
4 to 5 tablespoons sesame seeds
vegetable oil for frying
green onion pompom, to garnish

bread

vegetable oil

egg white

sesame seeds

gingerroot

sugar

shrimp

garlic

cornstarck

green onions

hot-pepper sauce

1 Put the first 9 ingredients in the bowl of a food processor and process until the mixture forms a smooth paste, scraping down the side of the bowl occasionally.

2 Spread the shrimp paste evenly over the bread slices, then sprinkle over the sesame seeds, pressing to make them stick. Remove the crusts, then cut each slice diagonally into 4 triangles, then cut each in half again to make 64 in total.

3 Heat 2 inches vegetable oil in a heavy saucepan or wok, until hot but not smoking. Fry the shrimp-coated triangles for 30 to 60 seconds, turning once. Drain on paper towels and serve hot.

COOK'S TIP

You can prepare these in advance and heat them up in a hot oven before serving. Make sure they are crisp and properly heated through though; they won't be nearly as enjoyable if there isn't any crunch!

Thai-Fried Vegetables in Wonton Cups

These crispy cups are an ideal way to serve stir-fried vegetables; use your imagination to vary the fillings.

Makes 24

INGREDIENTS

2 tablespoons vegetable oil, plus extra for greasing
24 small wonton wrappers
½ cup hoisin sauce or plum sauce (optional)
1 teaspoon sesame oil
1 garlic clove, finely chopped
½-inch piece fresh gingerroot, finely chopped
2-inch piece of lemongrass, crushed
6 to 8 asparagus spears, cut into 1¼-inch pieces
8 to 10 ears baby corn, cut in half lengthwise
1 small red pepper, seeded and cut into short slivers
1 to 2 tablespoons sugar
2 tablespoons soy sauce
juice of 1 lime
1 to 2 teaspoons Chinese-style chili sauce (or to taste)
1 tsp *huac nam* or Thai or other fish sauce

1 Preheat the oven to 350°F. Lightly grease twenty-four 1½-inch muffin cups. Press one wonton wrapper into each cup, turning the edges up to form a cup shape. Bake for 8 to 10 minutes until crisp and golden. Carefully remove to a wire rack to cool. If you like, brush each cup with a little hoisin or plum sauce (this will help keep the cups crisp if preparing them in advance).

2 In a wok or large skillet, heat 2 tablespoons vegetable oil and the sesame oil until very hot. Add the garlic, ginger, and lemongrass and stir-fry for 15 seconds until fragrant. Add the asparagus, corn, and red pepper pieces and stir-fry for 2 minutes until tender crisp.

3 Add the sugar, soy sauce, lime juice, chili sauce, and fish sauce and toss well to coat. Stir-fry for 30 seconds longer.

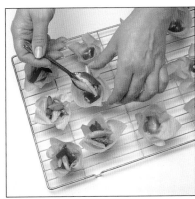

4 Spoon an equal amount of vegetable mixture into each of the prepared wonton cups and serve hot.

lemongrass

hoisin sauce

red pepper

wonton wrappers

baby corn

vegetable oil

asparagus

sesame oil

soy sauce

lime

garlic

Chicken Satay with Peanut Sauce

These skewers of marinated chicken can be prepared in advance and served at room temperature. Beef, pork, or even lamb tenderloin can be used instead of chicken, if you prefer.

Makes about 24

INGREDIENTS
1 pound boneless, skinless chicken
  breast halves
sesame seeds, for sprinkling
red pepper, to garnish

FOR THE MARINADE
6 tablespoons vegetable oil
4 tablespoons tamari or light soy
  sauce
4 tablespoons fresh lime juice
½-inch piece fresh gingerroot, peeled
  and chopped
3 or 4 garlic cloves
2 tablespoons light brown sugar
1 teaspoon Chinese-style chili sauce,
  or 1 small red chili pepper, seeded
  and chopped
2 tablespoons chopped fresh cilantro

FOR THE PEANUT SAUCE
2 tablespoons smooth peanut butter
2 tablespoons soy sauce
1 tablespoon sesame or vegetable oil
2 green onions, chopped
2 garlic cloves
1 to 2 tablespoons fresh lime or lemon
  juice
1 tablespoon brown sugar

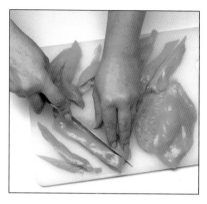

1 Prepare the marinade. Place all the marinade ingredients in the bowl of a food processor or blender and process until smooth and well blended, scraping down the sides of the bowl once. Pour into a shallow dish and set aside.

2 Into the same food processor or blender, put all the Peanut Sauce ingredients and process until well blended. If the sauce is too thick, add a little water and process again. Pour into a small bowl and cover until ready to serve.

3 Put the chicken breast halves in the freezer for 5 minutes to firm. Slice the meat in half horizontally, then into thin strips. Cut the strips into ¾-inch pieces.

4 Add the chicken pieces to the marinade in the dish. Toss well to coat, cover and marinate for 3 to 4 hours in a cool place, or overnight in a refrigerator.

5 Preheat the broiler. Line a cookie sheet with foil and brush lightly with oil. Thread 2 to 3 pieces of marinated chicken onto skewers and sprinkle with the sesame seeds. Broil for 4 to 5 minutes until golden, turning once. Serve with the Peanut Sauce, and a garnish of red pepper strips.

COOK'S TIP

When using metal skewers, look for flat ones which prevent the food from spinning around. If using wooden skewers, be sure to soak them in cold water for at least 30 minutes, to prevent them burning.

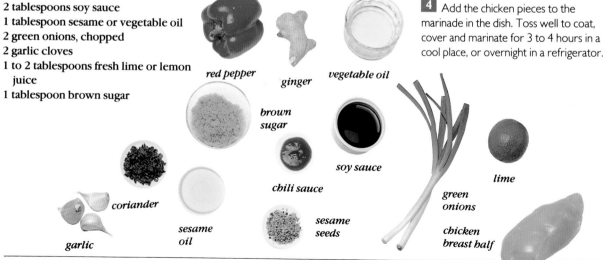

red pepper

ginger

vegetable oil

brown sugar

soy sauce

lime

coriander

chili sauce

green onions

garlic

sesame oil

sesame seeds

chicken breast half

Lamb Tikka

Creamy yogurt and nuts go wonderfully with
the spices in these little Indian meatballs.

Makes about 20

INGREDIENTS
1 pound lamb tenderloin
2 green onions, chopped

FOR THE MARINADE
1 ½ cups plain yogurt
1 tablespoon ground blanched
  almonds, cashews, or peanuts
1 tablespoon vegetable oil
2 or 3 garlic cloves, finely chopped
juice of 1 lemon
1 teaspoon garam masala or curry
  powder
½ teaspoon ground cardamom
¼ teaspoon cayenne pepper
1 to 2 tablespoons chopped fresh mint

1 Prepare the marinade. In a medium-size bowl, stir together all the ingredients except the lamb. In a separate small bowl, reserve about ½ cup of the mixture to use as a dipping sauce.

2 Cut the lamb into small pieces and put in the bowl of a food processor with the green onions. Process, using the pulse action until the meat is finely chopped. Add 2 to 3 tablespoons of the marinade and process again.

3 Test to see if the mixture holds together by pinching a little between your fingertips. Add a little more marinade if necessary, but do not make the mixture too wet and soft.

green onions

lamb tenderloin *ground almonds* *plain yogurt*

lemon *garam masala* *cayenne pepper*

ground cardamom *vegetable oil*

garlic

mint

4 With moistened palms, form the meat mixture into slightly oval-shaped balls about 1 ½ inches long and arrange in a shallow baking dish. Spoon over the remaining marinade, cover, and refrigerate the meatballs for 8 to 10 hours, or overnight.

5 Preheat the broiler and line a cookie sheet with foil. Thread each meatball onto a skewer and arrange on the cookie sheet. Broil for 4 to 5 minutes, turning occasionally, until crisp and golden on all sides. Serve with the reserved marinade/dipping sauce.

Smoked Duck Wontons with Spicy Mango Sauce

These Chinese-style wontons are easy to make using cooked smoked duck or chicken, or even left-over meat from Sunday lunch.

Makes about 40

INGREDIENTS
1 tablespoon light soy sauce
1 teaspoon sesame oil
2 green onions, finely chopped
grated peel of ½ orange
1 teaspoon brown sugar
1½ cups chopped smoked duck
about 40 small wonton wrappers
1 tablespoon vegetable oil

FOR THE SPICY MANGO SAUCE
2 tablespoons vegetable oil
1 teaspoon ground cumin
½ teaspoon ground cardamom
¼ teaspoon ground cinnamon
1 cup mango purée (about 1 large mango)
1 tablespoon honey
½ teaspoon Chinese chili sauce (or to taste)
1 tablespoon cider vinegar
snipped fresh chives, to garnish (optional)

1 Prepare the sauce. In a medium-size saucepan, heat the oil over medium-low heat. Add the spices and cook for about 3 minutes, stirring constantly.

2 Stir in the mango purée, honey, chili sauce, and vinegar. Remove from the heat and cool. Pour into a bowl and cover until ready to serve.

3 Prepare the wonton filling. In a large bowl, mix together the soy sauce, sesame oil, green onions, orange peel, and brown sugar until well blended. Add the duck and toss to coat well.

smoked duck

cardamom

cumin

cinnamon

sesame oil

mango

wonton wrappers

soy sauce

brown sugar

chili sauce

cider vinegar

green onions

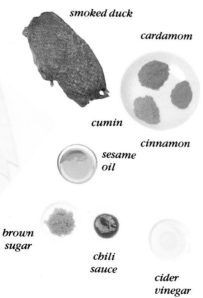

4 Place a teaspoonful of the duck mixture in the center of each wonton wrapper. Brush the edges lightly with water and then draw them up to the center, twisting to seal and forming a pouch shape.

5 Preheat the oven to 375°C. Line a large cookie sheet with foil and brush lightly with oil. Arrange the wontons on the cookie sheet and bake for 10 to 12 minutes until crisp and golden. Serve with the Spicy Mango Sauce. If you wish, tie each wonton with a fresh chive.

Tandoori Chicken Sticks

This aromatic chicken dish is traditionally baked in a special clay oven called a *tandoor*.

Makes about 25

INGREDIENTS

1 pound boneless, skinless chicken breast halves

FOR THE CILANTRO YOGURT

1 cup plain yogurt
2 tablespoons whipping cream
½ cucumber, peeled, seeded and finely chopped
1 to 2 tablespoons chopped fresh cilantro or mint
salt and freshly ground black pepper

FOR THE MARINADE

¾ cup plain yogurt
1 teaspoon garam masala or curry powder
¼ teaspoon ground cumin
¼ teaspoon ground cilantro
¼ teaspoon cayenne pepper (or to taste)
1 teaspoon tomato paste
1 or 2 garlic cloves, finely chopped
½-inch piece fresh gingerroot, peeled and finely chopped
grated peel and juice of ½ lemon
1 to 2 tablespoons chopped fresh cilantro or mint

chicken breast half   *cumin*

tomato paste   *garam masala*   *whipping cream*

garlic   *lemon*

1 Prepare the Cilantro Yogurt. Combine all the ingredients in a bowl and season with salt and freshly ground black pepper. Cover and refrigerate until ready to serve.

2 Prepare the marinade. Place all the ingredients in the bowl of a food processor and process until smooth. Pour into a shallow dish.

cucumber   *plain yogurt*

3 Freeze the chicken breasts for 5 minutes to firm, then slice in half horizontally. Cut the slices into ¾-inch strips and add to the marinade. Toss to coat well. Cover and refrigerate for 6 to 8 hours, or overnight.

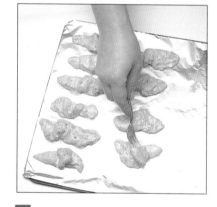

4 Preheat the broiler and line a baking sheet with foil. Using a slotted spoon, remove the chicken from the marinade and arrange the pieces in a single layer on the baking sheet. Scrunch up the chicken slightly so it makes wavy shapes. Grill for 4 to 5 minutes until brown and just cooked, turning once. Thread 1 or 2 pieces on to toothpicks or short skewers and serve with the yogurt dip.

Glazed Spareribs

These delicious sticky ribs are easy to eat with fingers once the little bones are cleaned away at one end to provide "handles."

Makes about 25

INGREDIENTS

2¼ pounds meaty pork spareribs, cut into 2-inch pieces
¾ cup tomato ketchup or mild chili sauce
2 to 3 tablespoons soy sauce
2 to 3 tablespoons honey
2 garlic cloves, finely chopped
¼ cup orange juice
¼ teaspoon cayenne pepper (or to taste)
¼ teaspoon Chinese five-spice powder
1 or 2 star anise

pork spareribs

orange juice

soy sauce

star anise

garlic

Chinese five-spice powder

honey

ketchup

cayenne pepper

1 Using a small sharp knife, scrape away about ¼ inch of meat from one end of each tiny sparerib to serve as a little "handle."

2 In a large bowl or shallow baking dish, mix together the ketchup or chili sauce, soy sauce, honey, garlic, orange juice, cayenne pepper, Chinese five-spice powder, and star anise until well blended. Add the ribs and toss to coat. Cover and refrigerate for 6 to 8 hours, or overnight.

3 Preheat the oven to 350°F. Line a baking tray with foil and arrange the spareribs in a single layer, spooning over any remaining marinade.

4 Bake, uncovered, basting occasionally, for 1 to 1½ hours, or until the ribs are well browned and glazed. Serve warm or at room temperature.

Sushi-style Tuna Cubes

These tasty tuna cubes are easier to prepare than classic Japanese sushi but retain the same fresh taste.

Makes about 24

INGREDIENTS
1½ pounds fresh tuna steak,
   ¾-inch thick
1 large red pepper, seeded and cut
   into ¾-inch pieces
sesame seeds for sprinkling

FOR THE MARINADE
1 to 2 tablespoons lemon juice
½ teaspoon salt
½ teaspoon sugar
½ teaspoon wasabi paste
½ cup olive or vegetable oil

FOR THE SOY DIPPING SAUCE
½ cup soy sauce
1 tablespoon rice wine vinegar
1 teaspoon lemon juice
1 or 2 green onions, finely chopped
1 teaspoon sugar
2 to 3 dashes Asian hot chili oil or
   hot-pepper sauce

soy sauce
fresh tuna
cilantro   *olive oil*
red pepper   *sesame seeds*
wasabi paste   *lemon juice*   *vinegar*
pepper sauce   *sugar*   *green onions*

1 Cut the tuna into 1-inch pieces and arrange them in a single layer in a large noncorrosive baking dish.

2 Prepare the marinade. In a small bowl, stir the lemon juice with the salt, sugar, and wasabi paste. Slowly whisk in the oil until well blended and slightly creamy. Stir in the cilantro. Pour over the tuna cubes and toss to coat. Cover and marinate for about 40 minutes in a cool place.

3 Meanwhile, prepare the Soy Dipping Sauce. Combine all the ingredients in a small bowl and stir until well blended. Cover until ready to serve.

4 Preheat the broiler and line a cookie sheet with foil. Thread a cube of tuna and then a piece of pepper onto each skewer and arrange on the cookie sheet.

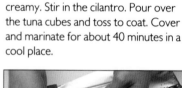

5 Sprinkle with sesame seeds and broil for 3 to 5 minutes, turning once or twice, until just beginning to color but still pink inside. Serve with the Soy Dipping Sauce.

COOK'S TIP

Wasabi is a hot, pungent Japanese horseradish available in powder form and as paste in a tube from gourmet and Japanese food stores.

Bombay Shrimp

These larger shrimp are expensive, so save this dish for a special occasion.

Makes 24

INGREDIENTS
¾ cup olive oil
1 teaspoon ground turmeric (or to taste)
1 teaspoon ground cumin
1 teaspoon garam masala or curry powder
½ teaspoon salt
½ teaspoon cayenne pepper (or to taste)
juice of 2 limes
24 large uncooked tiger or jumbo shrimp, shelled and deveined, tails attached
cilantro leaves, to garnish

limes

shelled shrimp

olive oil

turmeric   *cumin*

garam masala

cilantro

cayenne pepper

1 In a medium-sized bowl, whisk together well the oil, turmeric, cumin, garam masala, salt, cayenne pepper, and lime juice.

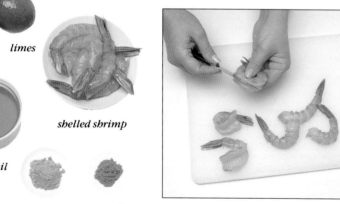

2 With a small sharp knife, slit three-quarters of the way through each shrimp, cutting down the center back (be careful not to cut right through). Add the shrimp to the marinade and allow to stand in a cool place for 40 minutes.

3 Preheat the broiler. Arrange the shrimp on a foil-lined broiler pan in a single layer. Drizzle a little of the marinade over. Broil for about 2 to 3 minutes until the shrimp are glazed and curled. Serve immediately, on toothpicks if you like, garnished with cilantro leaves.

COOK'S TIP

Wrap the shrimp tails in small pieces of foil to prevent them catching and burning under the broiler, then remove halfway through broiling. Make sure the shrimp are cooked through; test one by cutting in half.

Caramel Cape Gooseberries

These exotic fruits resemble shiny Chinese lanterns when dipped in golden caramel. Their tartness provides a perfect contrast to the sweetness of the coating.

Makes 24

INGREDIENTS
oil for greasing
24 Cape gooseberries
generous 1 cup granulated sugar
water

Cape gooseberries

sugar

1 Lightly oil a small cookie sheet. Carefully separate the papery leaves from the fruit of the Cape gooseberry and bend them back behind the berry, twisting them together at the stem.

2 Put the sugar in a small, heavy-bottomed saucepan, sprinkle with 2 to 3 tablepoons water and heat over low heat until the sugar melts, swirling the pan occasionally. Increase the heat to medium and bring to a boil. Boil for 4 to 5 minutes until the syrup turns a golden caramel color.

3 Dip the base of the pan in cold water to stop the cooking, then place it in a bowl of warm water so the caramel remains liquid. Be very careful, as the caramel can cause serious burns.

4 Holding each fruit by the papery leaves, carefully dip the berry into the caramel to coat completely. Set each fruit on the prepared baking sheet and allow to cool until hard.

INDEX

A

Almonds: mini macaroons, 29
Anchovies: carpaccio rolls with anchovy mayonnaise, 69
  crostini with three vegetable toppings, 38
Apples: straw potato cakes with caramelized apple, 44
Apricots, dried, 12
Artichokes: Italian-style marinated artichokes, 24
Asparagus: asparagus and Brie tartlets, 78
  grilled asparagus tips with easy hollandaise sauce, 74
Avocado: guacamole-filled cherry tomatoes, 47
  Scandinavian open-faced sandwiches, 60

B

Bacon: angels and devils on horseback, 46
  egg and bacon on fried bread, 48
  French country terrine, 58
Beef: carpaccio rolls with anchovy mayonnaise, 69
  hot salt beef on a stick, 33
  Scandinavian open-faced sandwiches, 60
Bombay mix, 12
Bombay shrimp, 94
Bread: egg and bacon on fried bread, 48
  Monti Cristo triangles, 57
  Scandinavian open-faced sandwiches, 60
  shrimp toasts, 82
Bread sticks, 12
  Prosciutto grissini, 26
Buffalo-style chicken wings, 53

C

Canelle knife, using, 17
Cape gooseberries: caramel Cape gooseberries, 95
Cashews, honey roast, 12
Caviar: scrambled egg and caviar tartlets, 78
Celery sticks with Roquefort, 24
Cheese: aromatic Greek olives with Feta, 26
  asparagus and Brie tartlets, 78
  blue-cheese dip, 53
  broiled Brie with walnuts, 40

celery sticks with Roquefort, 24
cheese balls, 37
cheese straws, 12
crostini with three vegetable toppings, 38
easy pesto sauce, 18
hazelnut sablés with goat cheese and strawberries, 80
hot crab dip, 34
medjol dates stuffed with cream cheese, 34
mini sausage rolls, 66
Monti Cristo triangles, 57
Parmesan phyllo triangles, 28
tiny cheese puffs, 42
Chicken: Buffalo-style chicken wings, 53
  chicken satay with peanut sauce, 84
  Monti Cristo triangles, 57
  Scandinavian open-faced sandwiches, 60
  tandoori chicken sticks, 90
Chicken livers: angels and devils on horseback, 46
Chickpeas: hummus, 62
Chili: chili flowers, 16
  easy nachos, 20
  hot and spicy popcorn, 22
Chocolate: rich chocolate and fruit fondue, 81
Condiments, 8
Corn: corn fritters with red pepper salsa, 64
Corned beef: hot corned beef on a stick, 33
Crab: hot crab dip, 34
  spicy crab cakes, 70
Cranberries, dried, 12
Crostini with three vegetable toppings, 38
Cucumber: smoked trout mousse in cucumber cups, 68
  twists, 16
  tzatziki, 62

D

Dates: medjol dates stuffed with cream cheese, 34
Dips: blue-cheese dip, 53
  easy Oriental dip, 30
  hot crab dip, 34
  smoky eggplant dip, 62
Drinks, 14
Duck: smoked duck wontons with spicy mango sauce, 88

E

Eggplant: smoky eggplant dip, 62
Eggs: egg and bacon on fried bread, 48
  Monti Christo triangles, 57
  scrambled egg and caviar tartlets, 78
  tortilla squares, 56

F

Fennel, slicing, 31
Fondue: rich chocolate and fruit fondue, 81
Fruit: rich chocolate and fruit fondue, 81

G

Garnishes, 16
Gherkins, 12
Greek meze with pita chips, 62
Grissini, 12
  Prosciutto grissini, 26

H

Ham: corn muffins with ham, 52
  Monti Cristo triangles, 57
Hazelnut sablés with goat cheese and strawberries, 80
Herbs, 9
  herb-stuffed mini-vegetables, 50
Hummus, 62

J

Japanese rice crackers, 12

L

Lamb tikka, 86
Leeks: French country terrine, 58
  smoked salmon and leek tartlets, 78
Lemon twists, 16

M

Macadamia nuts, 12
Mangoes: smoked duck wontons with spicy mango sauce, 88
Mayonnaise, 18
  carpaccio rolls with anchovy mayonnaise, 69
Muffins, corn muffins with ham, 52
Mussels: marinated mussels, 76

O

Olives, 12

aromatic Greek lives with Feta, 26
crostini with three vegetable toppings, 38
quick tapenade, 19
Onions: crostini with three vegetable toppings, 38
  green onion pompoms, 16

P

Pâtés and terrines, foie gras pâté in phyllo cups, 72
  French country terrine, 58
Peanuts: chicken satay with peanut sauce, 84
Pecans: hot pepper pecans, 20
Peppers: corn fritters with red pepper salsa, 64
  crostini with three vegetable toppings, 38
  roasting, 17
  slicing, 30
Pesto: easy pesto sauce, 18
Pistachios, 12
Pita chips, 12
Pizza: spicy sun-dried tomato pizza wedges, 54
Popcorn, 12
  hot and spicy popcorn, 22
Poppadums: spicy microwave poppadums, 22
Pork: French country terrine, 58
  glazed spareribs, 91
Potato chips, 12
Potatoes: mini baked potatoes with sour cream and chives, 36
  spicy baked potato boats, 40
  straw potato cakes with caramelized apple, 44
  tortilla squares, 56
Pretzel sticks, 12

R

Radish fans, 16
Rice: smoked salmon nests on wild rice pancakes, 71

S

Salmon: Scandinavian open-faced sandwiches, 60
Sausages: mini sausage rolls, 66
Scallops: angels and devils on horseback, 46
Shrimp crackers, 12
Shrimp: Bombay shrimp, 94
  shrimp toasts, 82

Smoked salmon: smoked salmon and leek tartlets, 78
  smoked salmon nests on wild rice pancakes, 71
Smoked trout mousse in cucumber cups, 68
Spices, 10
Store cupboard nibbles, 12
Strawberries: hazelnut sablés with goat cheese and strawberries, 80

T

Tandoori chicken sticks, 90
Tartlet tins, lining, 17
Thai-fried vegetables in wonton cups, 83
Tomatoes: basic tomato sauce, 19
  corn fritters with red pepper salsa, 64
  crostini with three vegetable toppings, 38
  guacamole-filled cherry tomatoes, 47
  spicy sun-dried tomato pizza wedges, 54
Tortellini kebabs, 32
Tortilla chips, 12
  easy nachos, 20
Tortilla squares, 56
Trio of tartlets, 78
Tuna: sushi-style tuna cubes, 92
Turkey: Monti Cristo triangles, 57
Tzatziki, 62

V

Vegetables: herb-stuffed mini-vegetables, 50
  Thai-fried vegetables in wonton cups, 83

W

Walnuts: broiled Brie with walnuts, 40
Wontons: smoked duck wontons with spicy mango sauce, 88
  Thai-fried vegetables in wonton cups, 83

Y

Yogurt: tzatziki, 62